Parish

of

Somerset

Records of Somerset County, Maryland

Saint Andrews Episcopal Church Princess Anne,
Saint Stephens Church in Potatoe Neck,
All Saints Church in Monie
and Grace Church, Wicomico Parish

Ruth T. Dryden

HERITAGE BOOKS
2008

HERITAGE BOOKS

AN IMPRINT OF HERITAGE BOOKS, INC.

Books, CDs, and more—Worldwide

For our listing of thousands of titles see our website
at
www.HeritageBooks.com

Published 2008 by
HERITAGE BOOKS, INC.
Publishing Division
100 Railroad Ave. #104
Westminster, Maryland 21157

International Standard Book Numbers
Paperbound: 978-1-58549-150-6
Clothbound: 978-0-7884-7620-4

Dedicated to

Lorenzo 2. Powell

without whose generosity

this book bould not have

been done

TABLE OF CONTENTS

(note:all names are recorded exactly as spelled in the text
of the orignial document)

These are records of the following Rectors

Rev. Henry Crosdale   -1838
Rev. James Ambercrobe   -1840
Rev. George McElhaney   -1840
Rev. John Crosdale   -1843-66
Rev. Harvey Stanley   -1844
Rev. Joseph J. Nicholson   -1849
Rev. Richard S. Killen   -1850
Rcv. Henry J. Windsor   -1851
Rev. William H. Hyland   -1851
Rev. William G. H. Jones   -1851
Rev. James Moore   -1852-58
Rev. William Augustus White -1853
Rev. Samuel K. Stewart   -1853
Rev. William T. Johnston   -1858
Rev. Charles S. Spencer   -1859
Rev. John O. Barton   -1862-86
Rev. John S. Miller   -1866
Rev. William Fulton   -1871
Rev. F. W. Hilliard   -1881
Rev. F. B. Adkins   -1883
Rev. O. H. Murphy   -1884

BIRTHS AND BAPTISMS

Hannah BENNETT d/o John BENNETT born at Manokin 20 October 1697

Stephen BENNETT s/o John BENNETT and Sarah BENNETT born 22 November 1699

Charles BANNISTER s/o William BANNISTER & Mary BANNISTER born at Annamessex 24 February 1697

William BANNISTER s/o William BANNISTER & Mary BANNISTER born 22 July 1699

Margaret BROWNE d/o John BROWNE & Agnice BROWNE born at Manokin 16 July 1699

William BROWNE s/o John BROWNE & Agnice BROWNE born at Manokin 23 September 1696

Thomas BROWNE s/o John BROWNE & Margrett BROWNE born at Manokin 28 October 1700

George BOZMAN s/o William BOZMAN & Katherine BOZMAN born 30 November 1712

William BOZMAN s/o William BOZMAN & Katherine BOZMAN born & December 1713

Isaac BOZMAN s/o George BOZMAN & Sarah BOZMAN born 28 June 1704

Sarah BOZMAN d/o George BOZMAN & Sarah BOZMAN born 18 March 1706/7

Bridget BOZMAN d/o George BOZMAN & Sarah BOZMAN born 15 January 1712

Betty BOZMAN d/o George BOZMAN & Sarah BOZMAN born 20 May 1714

George BOZMAN son of George BOZMAN & Sarah BOZMAN born 10 September 1717

Eleanor BOZMAN d/o William BOZMAN & Katherine BOZMAN born 12 Aug 1713

George BOZMAN s/o William BOZMAN & Katherine BOZMAN born 18 March 1717

William BURGIN s/o Daniel BURGIN & Mary BURGIN born 20 September 1720

Patrick BURGIN s/o Daniel BURGIN & Mary BURGIN born 12 March 1721/2

1

Rebecca BOZMAN d/o George BOZMAN & Mary BOZMAN born at Monie
31 December 1729

Sarah BURGIN d/o Daniel BURGIN & Mary BURGIN born at Goose
Creek 3 July 17--

Thomas CARY s/o William CARY & Mary CARY born July 1695

Elizabeth CARY d/o William CARY & Mary CARY born (no date)

Sary CARY d/o William CARY & Mary CARY born (no date)

James CANE s/o Godfrey CANE & Margrett CANE at Pocoson 28
February 1702

Ann CANE d/o Godfrey CANE & Margrett CANE born at Pocoson 14
March 1704/5

Benjamin COVINGTON s/o Thomas COVINGTON & Isabell COVINGTON
25 March 1716

Mary McCREADY d/o Andrew McCREADY & Mary McCREADY born 4
February 1723/4

Elizabeth DAVIS d/o Nathaniel DAVIS born at Back Creek 1
October 169-

Charles DAVIS s/o Nathaniel DAVIS born at Back Creek 1
August 1699

Mary DORMAN d/o Matthew DORMAN & Frances DORMAN born at
Wicomico 7 April 1701

Thomas DASHIELL s/o Thomas DASHIELL & Eliza DASHIELL born 30
June 1700

Henry DASHIELL s/o Thomas DASHIELL & Elizabeth DASHIELL born
23 March 1702/3

Matthew DORMAN son of Matthew DORMAN & Frances DORMAN born
28 November 1703

Michael DORMAN s/o Matthew DORMAN & Frances DORMAN born 23
September 1706

Charles DASHIELL s/o Thomas DASHIELL & Elizabeth DASHIELL
born 1 December 1705

Dorman HEATH s/o Abraham HEATH & Mary HEATH born at Manokin
on 29 January 1707

Levin DASHIELL s/o Thomas DASHIELL & Elizabeth DASHIELL born
22 February 1711

John DASHIELL s/o Thomas DASHIELL & Elizabeth DASHIELL born

22 February 1711

----- DORMAN s/o Henry DORMAN & Elizabeth DORMAN born 29
August 1714

Rachell DORMAN d/o Matthew DORMAN & Frances DORMAN born 30
August 1712

William DORMAN s/o Matthew DORMAN & Frances DORMAN born 5
Septmeber 1715

Agnis DORMAN d/o John DORMAN & Christian DORMAN born 16
October 1712

Hessey HATH d/o Abraham HATH & Mary HATH born 7 September
1711

Abraham HATH s/o Abraham HATH & Mary HATH born 6 May 1713

Hezekiah DORMAN s/o John DORMAN & Christian DORMAN born 26
April 1715

Thomas EVERTON s/o Thomas EVERTON & Jane EVERTON born at
Manokin 15 August 1697

Mary MALCOMB d/o Thomas MALCOMB & Bridget Hinson MALCOMB
born 30 January 1781

Whitty MALCOMB s/o Thomas MALCOMB & Bridget MALCOMB born 11
December 1783

Robert MALCOMB s/o John MALCOMB & Eleanor MALCOMB born 12
March 1755

Elias MALCOMB s/o John MALCOMB & Eleanor MALCOMB born 13
August 1756

Mary Elizabeth MALCOMB d/o John MALCOMB & Eleanor MALCOMB
born 16 February 1759

John MALCOMB s/o John MALCOMB & Eleanor MALCOMB born 12
October 1761

Levin MALCOMB s/o John MALCOMB & Eleanor MALCOMB born 9
March 1764

Edward MALCOMB s/o John MALCOMB & Eleanor MALCOMB born 16
August 1766.

Robert ELZEY s/o John ELZEY & Anne ELZEY born 2 July 1727

John ELZEY s/o Arnold ELZEY & Jane ELZEY born 20 November
1711

Arnold ELZEY s/o Arnold ELZEY & Jane ELZEY born 17 March

3

1713/14

William SASER s/o William SASER & Alice SASSER born at
Little Monie 31 May 1719

Arnold ELZEY s/o John ELZEY & Anne ELZEY born 2 October 1723

Bridget SASER d/o William SASER & Alie SASER born 29
December 1720

Ann SASER d/o same born 2 December 1722

Alice SASER d/o same born 3 July 1724

Benjamin SASER s/o William SASER & Alice SASER born 4
January 1725/6

Mary SASER d/o same born 4 June 1728

Robert LAWS s/o William LAWS of Robert LAWS of Money & wife
Bridget LAWS born 6 February 1740/1

George LAWS s/o William LAWS & Bridget LAWS born 3 November
1743

Elinor LAWS d/o William LAWS & Bridget LAWS born 15 November
1746

Mary LAWS d/o same born 12 January 1749

Elizabeth McCLEMMY d/o Whitty McCLEMMY & Sarah Waters
McCLEMMY born 19 June 1752

Easter McCLEMMY d/o same born 9 January 1755

Susanne McCLEMMY d/o same born 29 May 1759

Luke FOSKEE s/o Thomas FOSKEE & Valingtine FOSKEE born 16
November 1725

Sarah FISHER d/o John FISHER & Jane FISHER born at Manokin
24 April 1698 was baptized by George TROTTER minister and
John DONE, Sarah ELZEY & Ann BOZMAN were surities.

Elizabeth FURNICE d/o James FURNICE & Judith FURNICE born at
Manokin 29 August 1699

John FISHER s/o John FISHER & Jane FISHER born at Manokin 15
March 1700/1 was baptised by George TROTTER. William
TURPIN, John KING & Priscilla WHITTINGTON were surities.

Comfort FURNICE d/o James FURNICE & Judith FURNICE born at
Manokin 22 December 1701

William FISHER s/o John FISHER & Jane FISHER born at Manokin

24 February 1703/4 was baptized by George Keion minister.
Capt. Arnold ELZEY, Arnold ELZEY Jr. & Elizabeth ELZEY were
surieties.

Nicholas FOUNTAIN s/o Nicholas FOUNTAIN & Joanna FOUNTAIN
born at Back Creek 14 April 1704

Beraby FISHER s/o John FISHER & Jane FISHER born at Manokin
22 January 1706 was baptized by Alexander ADAMS minister.
John LAWS, Robert LAWS, Elinor ELZEY were surities

Samuel FOUNTAIN s/o Marcy FOUNTAIN & his second wife Mary
FOUNTAIN born 7 January 1707

Grace FOUNTAIN d/o Marcy FOUNTAIN & his first wife Mary
FOUNTAIN 5 December 1701

Sarah FOUNTAIN d/o Marcy FOUNTAIN & Mary FOUNTAIN born at
Back Creek 14 January 1708

William FEBUS s/o George FEBUS & Mary FEBUS born 13
September 1713/4

George COLLIER s/o John COLLIER & Ann Jones COLLIER born 22
November 1766

Thomas COLLIER s/o same born 19 December 1769 and died on 22
October 1770

Robert COLLIER s/o same born 15 June 1773

George IRVING s/o Thomas IRVING & Sarah IRVING born 7
November 1760
Sarah IRVING d/o same born 7 November 1762
Prisse IRVING d/o same born 19 October 1764
Joseph IRVING s/o same born 29 September 1766

Ann Denwood Gilliss IRVING d/o George IRVING & Ann IRVING
born 2 October 1786
John IRVING s/o same born 13 May 1790
Ephraim IRVING s/o same born 20 May 1792

Thomas HOBS s/o Joy HOBS & Mary HOBS born 14 December 1693
Elizabeth HOBS d/o same born 20 April 1697
Noble HOBS d/o same born 8 February 1698

Washington WALLER s/o William WALLER & Bridget WALLER born
25 February 1802 and baptized 9 April 1802 by Rev. John
PRICE

Lucretia Anne Eleanor McClester Elizabeth Gordon HANDY d/o
Richard H. HANDY & Elizabeth HANDY born 11 April 1802 was
baptized 13 April 1802 by Rev. John PRICE

Elen STAYTON d/o William STAYTON & Rebecca STAYTON who was

the daughter of Gowan WRIGHT born 17 June 1799

Leolin STAYTON s/o Levin STAYTON & wife Nelly STAYTON who
was the d/o Gowan WRIGHT & wife Ellen WRIGHT, born 15
December 1801

Ebenezer Handy Washington Levin Robert DASHIELL s/o John
DASHIELL & Polly DASHIELL born 16 October 1805

Henry POLK s/o Josiah POLK & Rebeccah POLK born 17 April
1807 and baptized on 31 May 1809 by Rev. James Kemp.

George Bozman WALLER s/o William WALLER & Bridget Bozman
WALLER born 27 August 1789

William WALLER s/o William WALLER & Bridget WALLER born 16
July 1791
James Diamond WALLER s/o same born 12 January 1793
Sally WALLER d/o same born 5 April 1795
Bridget WALLER d/o same born 22 September 1798
Washington WALLER s/o same born 28 February 1802
Elizabeth Ann WALLER d/o same born 26 April 1804

Thomas WHITE s/o Thomas & Mary WHITE born 25 April 1773

Sarah Ellen Staples WHITE d/o Thomas WHITE & Nancy WHITE
born 2 November 1798

Louise WHITE d/o same born 15 February 1800

Mary Ann WHITE d/o same born 7 December 1801

Thomas Gowan WHITE s/o same born 30 March 1804

Levin Curtis WHITE s/o same born 16 February 1806

John Robert LAWS s/o William LAWS & Amelia LAWS born 12 July
1810

Silas WHITE s/o Thomas WHITE & Nancy WHITE born 30 March
1808
Rebeccah Elizabeth WHITE d/o Thomas WHITE & Nancy WHITE born
3 February 1810

James WHITE s/o same born 5 August 1812

Matthias JONES s/o Dr. Matthias JONES & Milcah JONES born 25
May 1816 was baptized 25 March 1818

Thomas George ROBERTS s/o Benjamin ROBERTS & Elizabeth
ROBERTS born 23 September 1817 was baptized July 1818

Hamilton Wilmer WHITE s/o James WHITE & Biddy WHITE born 20
April 1817 was baptized 25 April 1818

Elizabeth Stewart HILL d/o Reubin HILL & Nancy HILL born 27
March 1818 was baptized July 1818

Susan Jane WILLIAMS d/o Benjamin WILLIAMS & Tabitha WILLIAMS
was baptized 12 September 1818

Mary Elizabeth BEAUCHAMP d/o James BEAUCHAMP & Amelia
BEAUCHAMP was baptized 13 September 1818

John Williams FURNISS, William Henry FURNISS, Edward
FURNISS, Mary Elizabeth Anne FURNISS children of Josiah
FURNISS & Nancy FURNISS were baptized July 1818

Carmilla JOHNSTON d/o John JOHNSTON & Mary JOHNSTON born 13
April 1818 was baptized September 1818

Eliza William WEBSTER d/o Jabez WEBSTER & Peggy WEBSTER born
30 March 1817 was baptized 25 October 1818

Mary Jane BLOODSWORTH d/o Littleton BLOODSWORTH & Sally
BLOODSWORTH born 14 September 1818 was baptized 25 October
1818.

Eleanor Anne LEATHERBY d/o Willis LEATHERBY & Anne LEATHERBY
born 29 January 1818 was baptized 11 November 1818

Travers HORNER s/o Benjamin HORNER & Rebecca HORNER born 20
May 1818 was baptized 25 October 1818

Mary Ann Margaret Elizabeth Sarah REICE d/o Joshua REICE was
baptized by Rev. Summers 1 May 1825

Virginia Helen REICE d/o Joshua REICE was baptized in March
1831 by Rev. McElhinney.

Margaret Ann BOWLAND d/o John N. BOWLAND & Susan BOWLAND
born 21 May 1825

Matthias MILES s/o Matthias MILES & Nancy MILES born 12 May
1825

Robert Henry MATTHEWS s/o Whittington MATTHEWS & Sally
MATTHEWS born 6 January 1819
Harriett MATTHEWS d/o same born 11 January 1823
Mary James MATTHEWS d/o same born 6 March 1825

James L. POLLITT s/o Littleton POLLITT & Maria POLLITT born
4 November 1825
Margaret Priscilla POLLITT d/o same born 16 August 1826
William POLLITT s/o same born 4 Febraury 1827

Sarah Avery COVELL d/o Rev. Joseph COVELL & Eliza COVELL
born 3 February 1827

Edward PEARCE s/o Gideon PEARCE & Elizabeth PEARCE born 18--

Charles H. JONES s/o Levin JONES & Matilda JONES born 20 September 1827

Littleton C. LONG s/o Littleton & Mary LONG born 15 September 1827

Mary H. R. HARRIS d/o Littleton HARRIS & Mary HARRIS born 3 May 1827

John Harris WHITELOCK s/o James WHITELOCK & Harriet WHITELOCK born 3 August 1825
Matilda Jane WHITELOCK d/o same born 27 September 1827
Priscilla Amanda WHITELOCK d/o same born 27 September 1827

Juliana Margaret JONES d/o William JONES & Juliana Jones born 27 August 1827

William L. JONES s/o Dr. William JONES & Margaret JONES born 6 December 1827

Thomas W. HOLBROOK s/o Samuel HOLBROOK & Priscilla HOLBROOK born 25 June 1827

Albert A. WALLER s/o George WALLER & Eleanor WALLER born 27 April 1827

Joseph SUDLER s/o Joseph & Henrietta SUDLER born 28 July 1828

Aurelia KING d/o John H. KING & Sally E. G. KING born 6 August 1828

William Tilghman JOHNSTON s/o William W. JOHNSTON & Elizabeth JOHNSTON born 25 October 1830 was baptized April 1831 by Rev. George McELHINNEY.

John Woolford POLK s/o William T. G. POLK & Eliza POLK was baptized 28 June 1835 by Rev. William PICKNEY

William Woolford POLK s/o same was baptized 13 July 1835

Henry Raymond Judah REICE s/o Joshua REICE was baptized 5 August 1835 by Rev. William PICKEY

Anne Mary WILKINS d/o Washington WILKINS was baptized 5 August 1835

James Diamond WALLER s/o Washington WALLER was baptized 5 August 1835

William Thomas WHITE s/o Levin WHITE was baptized 5 August 1835.

Robert James COULBOURN d/o Robert H. COULBOURN was baptized 16 August 1835

8

Rufus P. JONES s/o John JONES was baptized 2 September 1835

Matthew TAYLOR s/o Samuel TAYLOR & Leah TAYLOR born 30 July 1795 was baptized 27 March 1796

Nancy Dougherty JENKINS d/o Joshua JENKINS & Mary Ann JENKINS born 10 October 1795 was baptized 27 March 1796

John COVINGTON son of Nehemiah COVINGTON & Ann COVINGTON born 27 March 1796 was baptized 3 April 1796

Leah Ann Whittington KING d/o Whittington KING & Nancy KING was born 2 August 1795 was baptized 3 April 1796

Polly KING d/o Samuel KING & Leah KING born 20 December 1795 was baptized 10 April 1796

John ADAMS s/o John H. ADAMS & Leah ADAMS born 22 Feb 1796 was baptized 17 April 1796

Betsey HORNER d/o Benjamin HORNER & Elizabeth HORNER born 1 November 1795 was baptized 10 March 1796

Nelly MEZICK d/o Elihu MEZICK & Leah MEZICK born 29 November 1795 was baptized 10 March 1796

George McDORMAN s/o Archer McDORMAN & Betsy McDORMAN born 31 January 1796 was baptized 22 May 1796

John LEATHERBURY s/o of Robert LEATHERBURY & Elizabeth LEATHERBURY born 1 October 1795 was baptized 5 June 1795

Millie HARLOW s/o David HARLOW & Sarah HARLOW born 24 February 1796 was baptized 5 June 1796

Sarah Leander JONES d/o Phillip JONES & Margaret JONES born 30 December 1795 was baptized 10 July 1796

Planner KING s/o Levin KING & Peggy KING born 4 June 1796 was baptized 21 August 1796

William GIBBONS son of Ezekiel GIBBONS & Polly GIBBONS born 3 June 1796 was baptized 20 August 1796

Elizabeth CUMLESS d/o Thomas Gilbert CUMLESS and Inda CUMLESS born 31 May 1795 was baptized 15 October 1796

John DISHAROON s/o Newton DISHAROON & Mary DISHAROON born 25 September 1796 was baptized 28 May 1797

Tubman JONES s/o Thomas JONES & Betsy JONES born 29 October 1796 was baptized 14 August 1797

Betsy POLLITT d/o David POLLITT & Sarah POLLITT born 14 November 1796 was baptized 25 May 1797

9

Esme Bayly DONE d/o John DONE & Patience DONE born 13
January 1797 was baptized 14 June 1797

Henrietta Ann Elzey BALLARD d/o William BALLARD & Eleanor
BALLARD born 1 October 1796 was baptized 30 April 1797

Stehen Disharoon BAYLY s/o Obed BAYLY & Leah BAYLY born 29
November 1796 was baptized 25 May 1797

Joseph Merrritt PUSEY s/o John PUSEY and Sarah Evans PUSEY
born 7 September 1796 was baptized 20 March 1797

James SHORES s/o Levin SHORES & Bridget SHORES born 17 March
1797 was baptized.

Sally SIMPKINS d/o Charles SIMPKINS & Naomy SIMPKINS born 17
November 1796 was baptized 7 June 1797

John COVINGTON s/o Thomas COVINGTON & Elizabeth COVINGTON
born 22 March 1797 was baptized 18 June 1797

Robert JONES s/o George JONES & Leah JONES born 13 November
1796 was baptized 25 June 1797

Nancy ODEAR d/o Bosman ODEAR & Nancy ODEAR born 22 January
1796 was baptized 25 June 1797

Nelly REID d/o Ballard REID and Nanney´REID born 24 April
1797 was baptized 18 June 1797

Peggy GIBBONS d/o Robert GIBBONS and Sarah GIBBONS born 28
January 1797 was baptized 20 August 1797.

Sarah WHITE d/o Matthew WHITE & William WHITE born 22 May
1797 was baptized 14 July 1797

Richard McLEAN s/o Enoch McLEAN and Elizabeth McLEAN born 18
January 1797 was baptized 23 July 1797

Leah MALCOMB d/o Peggy MALCOMB born 28 Febraury 1797 was
baptized 13 August 1797

Priscilla GIBBONS d/o William GIBBONS & Ann GIBBONS born 14
June 1797 was baptized 3 September 1797

Thomas SMITH s/o Fairfax SMITH and Rebecca SMITH born 23
June 1797 was baptized 17 September 1797

Matilda Waters DONE d/o William DONE & Peggy DONE born 12
July 1797 was baptized 17 September 1797

Lishey POLLITT d/o William POLLITT & Lishey born 31 January
1797 was baptized 17 September 1797

Nancy WEBSTER d/o Jabus WEBSTER & Polly WEBSTER born 5 May 1797 was baptized 14 July 1797

Elizabeth CROCKETT d/o John CROCKETT & Nancy CROCKETT was baptized 13 August 1797

George BALLARD s/o Jarvis BALLARD & Sarah BALLARD born 11 January 17997 was baptized 15 July 1797

John BOWEN s/o William BOWEN & Nancy BOWEN born 7 August 1793 was baptized 30 July 1797

Peggy GIBBONS d/o Robert GIBBONS & Sarah GIBBONS born 20 June 1797 was baptized 20 August 1797

Charles WILSON s/o John WILSON & Polly Abbott WILSON born 9 February 1797 was baptized 8 September 1797

Matilda Waters DONE d/o William DONE & Peggy DONE born 12 July 1797 was baptized 17 September 1797

Lishey POLLITT d/o William POLLITT & Lishey POLLITT born 31 January 1797 was baptized 17 September 1797

Thomas SMITH s/o Fairfax SMITH & Rebecca SMITH born 23 June 1797 was baptized 17 September 1797

John Whittington KING s/o Whittington KING & Nancy KING born 27 September 1797 was baptized 21 January 1798

Joshua HAYMAN s/o Isaac HAYMAN & Rebecca HAYMAN born 7 March 1797 was baptized

William HEATH s/o John HEATH & Nancy HEATH born 27 August 1797 was baptized 11 February 1798

Betsy Henry Bell KING d/o Levin KING & Peggy KING born 20 October 1797 was baptized 4 March 1798

Gilbert LAWES s/o William LAWES & Sarah LAWES born 24 August 1797 was baptized 11 March 1798

John JONES s/o George JONES & Peggy JONES born 10 August 1797 was baptized

Rachel LOWE d/o Ralph LOWE & Ellendor LOWE born 17 February 1798 was baptized 21 March 1798

George Tull BROWN s/o David BROWN Jr. & Annie BROWN born 22 January 1797 was baptized 15 April 1797

Polly Collins HITCH d/o John HITCH & Jeanie HITCH born 27 November 1797 was baptized 1 April 1798

Levin Dashiell PARKER s/o John Parker & Nancy Parker born 26

September 1797 was baptized 1 April 1798

Sarah MOREL d/o Michael MOREL & Mary MOREL born 24 December 1797 was baptized

Thomas HITCH s/o John HITCH & Milly HITCH born 8 October 1797 was baptized 29 April 1798

Harriett Bell SAVAGE d/o Ezekiel SAVAGE & Jane SAVAGE born 21 February 1797 was baptized 13 May 1798

Elizabeth MATTHEWS d/o Joseph MATTHEWS & Polly MATTHEWS born 18 September 1797 was baptized 13 July 1798

Eunice JONES d/o Levin JONES & Elizabeth JONES born 23 September 1797 was baptized 6 May 1798

William Wilson JOHNSON s/o George JOHNSON & Peggy JOHNSON born July 1797 was baptized

Matty HAYMAN d/o Randal HAYMAN & Polly HAYMAN born 29 October 1797 was baptized 10 June 1798

Crecy TAYLOR d/o Samuel TAYLOR & Leah TAYLOR born 28 February 1798 was baptized 10 June 1798

Jenny MORRIS d/o Jacob MORRIS & Sarah MORRIS born 25 March 1798 was baptized 10 June 1798

John Holbrook MORRISS s/o John MORRISS & Priscilla MORRIS born 30 June 1797 was baptized 27 April 1798

Clarissa STEWART d/o John STEWART & Jane STEWART born 17 March 1787
James STEWART d/o John STEWART & Jane STEWART born 14 November 1788
Elizabeth Ann STEWART d/o same born 11 September 1790
Jane Clarissa STEWART d/o same born 21 December 1792
John Henry STEWART s/o same born 19 February 1795
Nelly STEWART d/o same born 25 August 1796
Sally STEWART d/o same born 10 January 1798

William WILSON s/o John WILSON born 20 May 1798 was baptized 1 July 1798

Doly WATERS d/o James WATERS & Peggy WATERS born 7 March 1798 was baptized 1 July 1798

John JONES s/o John JONES & Sally JONES born 1 May 1798 was baptized 8 July 1798

Ann KELLEY d/o John KELLEY & Sarah KELLEY born 4 December 1797 was baptized 8 July 1798

Jesse PARKS s/o Arthur PARKS & Mary PARKS born 19 July 1797

12

was baptized 8 July 1798

Sarah BLOODSWORTH d/o Robert BLOODSWORTH born 23 December
1797 was baptized 8 July 1798

William BLAKE s/o Daniel BLAKE & Mary BLAKE born 31 August
1797 was baptized 8 July 1798

Francis WHITE s/o Francis WHITE & Grace WHITE born 26 July
1797 was baptized 8 July 1798

John Dashiell JONES s/o William JONES & Eunice JONES born 15
January 1798 was baptized 11 July 1798

Polly OWENS d/o James OWENS & Sally OWENS born 28 March 1798
was baptized 22 July 1798

James MILES s/o George MILES & Bridget MILES born 1 April
1798 was baptized 22 July 1798

Elizabeth Ann BALLARD d/o Daniel BALLARD & Dolly BALLARD
born 2 June 1798 was baptized 29 July 1798

Gabriel BANKS s/o Warren BANKS & Nancy BANKS born 22 January
1798 was baptized 9 August 1798

George MAGEE s/o George & Nancy MAGEE born 6 March 1798 was
baptized 9 August 1798

Thomas Prior MALCOMB d/o Edward MALCOMB & Elizabeth MALCOMB
born 3 May 1798 was baptized 12 Aug 1798

Nancy Adams FORD d/o Gilbert FORD & Hester FORD born 18
April 1798 was baptized 19 August 1798
Anthony Zadock DeBORME s/o Anthony DeBORME & Sarah DeBORME
born 10 April 1798 was baptized 19 August 1798

Mary HOPKINS d/o Richard HOPKINS & Elizabeth HOPKINS born 5
January 1798 was baptized 26 Septembr 1798

Matilda HYLAND d/o Lambert HYLAND & Sarah HYLAND born 5 July
1798 was baptized 2 October 1798

Polly HARLON d/o David HARLON & Sarah HARLON born 17 August
1798 was baptized 22 October 1798

Peggy Irving WROTTEN d/o John WROTTEN & Catherine WROTTEN
born 8 September 1798 was baptized 22 October 1798

John Planner GALE d/o John GALE & Amelia GALE born 21
November 1797 was baptized 16 September 1798

Nancy HAYMAN d/o William HAYMAN & Esther HAYMAN born 21
November 1797 was baptized 23 Nov 1798

Sally Rigby MADDUX d/o William MADDUX and Leah MADDUX born 5 October 1798 was baptized 25 October 1798

Bridget WALLER d/o William WALLER & Bridget WALLER born 22 September 1798 was baptized 18 November 1798

Nelly WILSON d/o David WILSON & Sally WILSON born 14 November 1798 was baptized 3 Jan 1799

Amelia MILYKIN d/o John MILYKIN & Sally MILYKIN born 15 December 1798 was baptized 3 January 1799

John GLASGO s/o James GLASGO & Betsy GLASGO born 17 May 1798 was baptized 3 January 1799

James McDORMAN s/o George McDORMAN & Betsy McDORMAN born 13 July 1798 was baptized

Francis DISHAROON s/o Edward DISHAROON & Hetty DISHAROON born 13 June 1798 was baptized

Polly PRICE d/o Kibble PRICE & Betsy PRICE born 15 July 1798 was baptized 11 November 1798

Betsey ANDERSON d/o William ANDERSON & Polly ANDERSON born 25 November 1798 was baptized 22 January 1799

Sarah DAVIS d/o Elzey DAVIS & Mary DAVIS born 1 December 1798 was baptized 9 June 1799

Henry MATTHIS s/o John MATTHIS & Edy MATTHIS born 7 November 1798 was baptized 9 June 1799

Mary Henrietta Hayward Wilson PERRY d/o Ishmael PERRY & Peggy PERRY born 20 October 1798 was baptized 25 May 1799

James JONES s/o Levin JONES & Eliza JONES born February 1799 was baptized 2 June 1799

Isaac BOZMAN d/o David BOZMAN & Susannah BOZMAN born 6 November 1798 was baptized 2 June 1799

William Upshur MAGRATH s/o John MAGRATH & Anne MAGRATH born 8 January 1799 was baptized 26 May 1799

Robert DONE & Mary Hayward DONE son and daughter of William DONE & Peggy DONE were born 12 November 1798 were baptized 5 February 1799

Susan Walker SMITH d/o Fairfax SMITH & Rebecca Enols SMITH born 26 October 1798 was baptized 21 April 1799

Prissey KELLY d/o John KELLY & Sarah KELLY born 8 March 1799 was baptized 2 April 1799

14

William Gorah KING s/o Samuel KING & Leah KING born 1
February 1799 was baptized 2 June 1799

David WHITE s/o William WHITE & Martha WHITE born 21
November 1798 was baptized 3 April 1799

James WALLACE s/o James & Mary WALLACE born 12 March 1799
was baptized 5 April 1799

Elizabeth WINDSOR d/o Henry WINDSOR born 2 January 1799 was
baptized 5 March 1799

Betsy POLLITT d/o John POLLITT & Mary POLLITT born 11 July
1798

Fielder AUSTIN s/o Isaac AUSTIN & Martha AUSTIN born 22
January 1799 was baptized 5 May 1799

Henrietta Maria INSLEY d/o John INSLEY and Amelia INSLEY
born 10 July 1798 was baptized 3 April 1799

Sarah HOBBS d/o Benjamin HOBBS & Rebecca HOBBS born 19 June
1798 was baptized 3 March 1799

Priscilla WHITNEY d/o Joseph WHITNEY and Ann WHITNEY born 11
October 1798 was baptized 13 February 1799

Elizabeth Ann SMITH d/o Benjamin SMITH & Sarah Ann SMITH
born 29 October 1798 was baptized 7 April 1799

Sarah Ellen Hughes WHITE d/o Thomas WHITE & Ann WHITE born 2
November 1798 was baptized 24 March 1799

Bridget JONES d/o John JONES & Sarah JONES born 24 July 1798
was baptized 17 April 1799

Betsey DURHAM d/o Thomas DURHAM & Zella DURHAM born 9
September 1798 was baptized 9 June 1799

John Bloodsworth CURTIS s/o Thomas CURTIS & Peggy CURTIS
born 31 October 1798 was baptized 25 May 1799

William Hamilton KING s/o John KING & Harriett KING born 18
January 1800 was baptized 27 June 1800

Samuel Gillis HOLBROOK s/o Samuel HOLBROOK & Nelly Dashiell
HOLBROOK born 26 November 1799 was baptized 27 June 1800

Tubman LOWES s/o William LOWES & Sarah LOWES born 4 February
1800 was baptized 27 June 1800

Peggy WHITE d/o William WHITE & Nancy WHITE born 31 October
1799 was baptized 27 June 1800

Charlotte Whittington KING d/o Whittington KING & Nancy KING born 24 May 1800 was baptized 27 June 1800

Alexander BOZMAN d/o William BOZMAN & Betsy BOZMAN born 4
November 1799 was baptized 27 June 1800

Maria Washington KING d/o Levin KING & Peggy KING born 14
December 1799 was baptized 27 June 1800

Sally DASHIELL d/o Henry DASHIELL & Jane DASHIELL born 1
August 1800 was baptized 9 November 1800

Samuel STEVENS s/o William STEVENS born 5 August 1800 was
baptized 9 November 1800

George James JONES d/o Levin JONES & Eliza JONES born 20
November 1800 was baptized 24 May 1801

Thomas NEWMAN s/o Isaac NEWMAN & Polly NEWMAN born 9 Dcember
1800 was baptized 24 May 1901

Henry Upshur BALLARD d/o Levin BALLARD & Sarah BALLARD born
30 December 1800

Levin Rattcliffe HOBBS s/o Matthias HOBBS & Esther HOBBS
born 15 February 1801 was baptized 31 May 1801

Jenny ONIONS d/o James ONIONS & Sally ONIONS born 25
December 1800

Joseph MURPHY s/o Isaac MURPHY & Betsy MURPHY born 16 May
1801

Peggy Revel d/o David REVEL & Sally REVEL born 19 June 1801

Elizabeth TEACKLE d/o Littleton D. TEACKLE & Elizabeth
TEACKLE born 4 February 1801 was baptized 6 February 1801

Jane Dashiell Robertson STEWART d/o John STEWART & Jane
STEWART born 31 July 1801 was baptized 6 September 1801

William REVEL s/o John REVEL & Sarah REVEL born 19 January
1801

Meriah Jones REVEL s/o William REVEL & Nancy REVEL born 13
March 1801

Nancy GIBBONS d/o James GIBBONS & Amelia GIBBONS born 29
October 1800

Levin JONES s/o Charles JONES & Hetty JONES born 13 May 1801

Polly McDORMAN d/o Archey McDORMAN & Elizabeth McDORMAN born
21 February 1801

Betsy Hayman HOBBS d/o Thomas HOBBS & Sarah HOBBS born 16

November 1800 was baptized 10 May 1801

Ann Bannister MOOR d/o John MOOR & Sally MOOR born 1 March 1801

John Holbrook JONES s/o George JONES & Leah JONES born 5 April 1801

John Shiles HASKELL d/o John HASKELL & Nancy HASKELL born 24 May 1801

Elizabeth HARRIS d/o William HARRIS & Eby HARRIS born 10 June 1801

Thomas WHITE s/o William WHITE & Martha WHITE born 1 December 1800

Levin Malcomb CUSTIS s/o Isaac CUSTIS born 12 June 1801

Edwin LOWES s/o Thomas LOWES & Nelly LOWES born 7 December 1801 was baptized 9 April 1802 by Rev. John PRICE

Leah Matilda STEWART d/o John STEWART & Jane STEWART born 19 November 1805

William James POLK s/o Josiah POLK & Rebeccah POLK born 5 January 1809 was baptized 31 May 1809 by Rev. James KEMP

Sarah Hannah CURTIS d/o William H. CURTIS & Mary M. CURTIS born 12 December 1835 was baptized 3 August 1836

Samuel POLK d/o William T. POLK & Elizabeth POLK born 15 July 1836 was baptized 21 August 1836

Margaret Esther STEWART d/o James STEWART & Molly G. H. STEWART born 15 January 1836 was baptized 25 January 1836

Mary Eleanora JONES d/o William C. E. JONES & Sally A. E. JONES born 25 November 1835 was baptized 22 August 1835

Virginia Caroline JONES d/o Robert V. JONES & Eleanor A. JONES born 3 February 1836 was baptized 5 November 1836

Ellen Rebecca JOHNSTON d/o William W. JOHNSTON & Rosina M. JOHNSTON born 25 May 1836 was baptized 1 July 1836

Jane Wallis JONES infant d/o William H. JONES & Jane JONES was baptized 4 January 1838

Louisa Virginia WHITE and Sarah Helen WHITE daughters of Levin C. WHITE & Eliza Anne WHITE born 14 August 1837 were baptized 21 March 1838

John Done KING s/o John H. KING & Charlotte KING born 31 August 1836 was baptized 8 May 1838

John Custis HANDY s/o Littleton D. HANDY & Sophia HANDY born 2 February 1838 was baptized 25 May 1838

Susan Upshur JOHNSTON d/o William W. JOHNSTON & Rosina M. JOHNSTON born 2 October 1837 was baptized 10 June 1838

John Sydney SMITH s/o John SMITH and Mary W. SMITH born 4 April 1837 was baptized 24 June 1838

Sarah Elizabeth Maria WALLER d/o George WALLER & Nelly WALLER born 20 May 1838 was baptized 8 July 1838

Rebecca Whitney TULL born 9 May 1834, Sarah Elizabeth Ellen TULL born 29 December 1835 and Daniel James TULL born 14 November 1837 children of William M. TULL & Susan E. TULL were baptized 11 July 1838

Henry Page CRISFIELD infant s/o J. Woodland CRISFIELD and Ethelen CRISFIELD was baptized 13 July 1838

John Trippe HANDY s/o John L. HANDY & Elizabeth T. HANDY born 24 June 1837 was baptized 13 October 1838

William Francis MILLER s/o John MILLER & Maria MILLER born 25 October 1838 was baptized 21 April 1839

Susan Dixon BOWLAND born 19 January 1830, Sydney Grandison BOWLAND born 10 October 1832, Sally Lane BOWLAND born 5 February 1835, Amanda Adeline BOWLAND born 14 June 1838 children of John N. BOWLAND & Susan BOWLAND were baptized 22 April 1839

Addison Mortimer LONG son of Littleton LONG and Anne M. LONG was born 5 May 1838 was baptized 5 May 1838

Alexander Sydney CROCKETT s/o William B. CROCKETT & Ann CROCKETT born 25 September 1838 was baptized 19 May 1838

Henreitta Maria HYLAND d/o James C. HYLAND & Mary HYLAND born 12 July 1838 was baptized 20 July 1838

Alexander FURNISS s/o Ephraim FURNISS & Mary FURNISS born 20 July 1839 was baptized 14 September 1839

Mary Ratcliffe INGERSOLL born 16 December 1829, Georgiana INGERSOLL born 7 January 1833 daughters of Thomas INGERSOLL & Ann INGERSOLL were baptized 14 Septmeber 1838

Emily Upshur JOHNSTON d/o William W. JOHNSTON & Rosina M. JOHNSTON born 30 March 1839 was baptized 29 September 1839

Henry Clay RENSCHER born 20 January 1837, Matilda Victoria RENSCHER born 19 September 1839 children of Harry RENSCHER & S. RENSCHER were baptized 9 November 1838

John Wesley CARVIN s/o John CARVIN & Mary CARVIN born 12 November 1836 was baptized 9 March 1840

Lelote Washington CARVIN d/o John CARVIN & Mary CARVIN born 17 April 1838 was baptized 9 March 1840

James Henry CARVIN s/o John & Mary CARVIN born 14 February 1840 was baptized 9 March 1840

Edward Walton LEWIS s/o James LEWIS & Nancy LEWIS born 1 April 1839 was baptized 12 March 1840

William Edward LONG s/o Samuel W. LONG & Rachel LONG born 28 December 1839 was baptized 19 March 1840

Mary STEWART d/o James STEWART & Nelly STEWART born 22 February 1840 was baptized 20 May 1840

Ann Thoms WALLER d/o Washington WALLER & Mary Ann WALLER born 23 July 1839 was baptized 12 July 1839

Ariana Frazier JONES d/o Samuel W. JONES & Sally R. JONES born 31 May 1839 was baptized 15 July 1840

Wilhemina RENCHER d/o George Hitch RENCHER & Mary RENCHER born 16 November 1839 was baptized 9 August 1840

Granville Graham GARDINER s/o Mrs. Henrietta GARDNER born 15 April 1840 was baptized 25 November 1840

Joseph Stewart COTTMAN s/o Joseph L. COTTMAN & Elizabeth COTTMAN born 13 February 1839 was baptized 1 December 1840

Elizabeth Dennis COTTMAN d/o Joseph L. COTTMAN & Elizabeth COTTMAN born 30 August 1836 was baptized 1 December 1840

Levin Prettyman WHITE s/o Levin C. WHITE & Eliza Ann White born 22 February 1840 was baptized 3 January 1841

Betsy Gale JONES d/o William H. JONES & Sarah JONES born 20 July 1840 was baptized 7 March 1841

Mary Elizabeth WALTON born 28 March 1821 d/o William WALTON & Annie WALTON was baptized 22 April 1841

John Samuel MILLER s/o John MILLER & Maria MILLER born 27 November 1840 was baptized 5 June 1841

Ellen STEWART d/o John H. STEWART & Mary G. STEWART born 7 February 1841 was baptized 20 June 1841

Mary Gale HYLAND born 2 June 1836 and Harriett Elizabeth HYLAND born 5 November 1839 children of Henry HYLAND & Harriett HYLAND were baptized 20 June 1841

Henrietta Elzey Jones HUGHES d/o Josiah HUGHES & Louisa HUGHES born 14 January 1841 was baptized 3 July 1841

Maria Louisa Villars TULL d/o William M. TULL & Susan TULL born 12 December 1839 was baptized 17 July 1841

George Upshur JOHNSTON s/o William W. JOHNSTON & Rosina M. JOHNSTON born 13 April 1841 was baptized 29 August 1841

Louis Littleton McGRATH s/o Louis Upshur McGRATH & Rachel McGRATH born 26 June 1841 was baptized 9 September 1841

John Smith JONES s/o George JONES & Rebecca JONES born 24 January 1841 was baptized 9 October 1841

George Smith DASHIELL s/o Samuel DASHIELL & Mary Ellen DASHIELL born 3 December 1841 was baptized 22 April 1842

Sarah Esther Hough Bishop COTTMAN d/o Joseph S. COTTMAN & Elizabeth COTTMAN born 13 January 1841 was baptized 28 April 1842

Gustavious Wright WHITE s/o James WHITE & Adeline WHITE born 10 January 1841 was baptized 8 May 1842

Mary Washington WALLER d/o Washington WALLER & Mary Ann WALLER born 1 August 1841 was baptized 8 May 1842

Francies Virginia Crosdale WHITNEY d/o James WHITNEY & Ann WHITNEY born 31 January 1841 was baptized 30 July 1842

Thomas Henry Keppler BAYLY born 11 July 1840, Stephen Alfred BAYLY born 5 March 1842 children of Elias BAYLY & Elenaor BAYLY were baptized 10 September 1842

Charles Rollinson Whittingham LONG s/o Litttleton LONG & Ann M. LONG born 2 July 1842 was baptized 10 September 1842

Ellen Henry WHITELOCK born 12 August 1824 was baptized 6 November 1842

Elizabeth JONES born 6 October 1825 was baptized 20 December 1842

Sarah JOHNSTON, do William W. JOHNSTON & Rosina M. JOHNSTON born 25 December 1842 was baptized 1 January 1843

Maria Elizabeth WATERS born 15 December 1837, Arnold Elzey Waters born 1 October 1839, Romanoff Baker WATERS born 1

February 1841, William George WATERS born 3 November 1843 children of William Elzey WATERS and Anna Maria WATERS were baptized 29 February 1844

Henrietta GRACE Miller infant d/o John MILLER & Maria MILLER was baptized 5 May 1844

Susan Esther DAUGHERTY d/o John DAUGHERTY & Mary DAUGHERTY born 14 December 1843 was baptized 10 May 1844

Henrietta Jones STEWART infant d/o John H. STEWART & Mary G. STEWART was baptized 13 July 1844

Samuel JONES infant s/o Samuel W. JONES & Sally R. JONES was baptized 13 July 1844

Henrietta Matilda Maria Wilson JONES d/o Samuel W. JONES & Sally JONES was baptized 13 July 1844

Charles DORSEY infant s/o Thomas DORSEY & Ellen DORSEY was baptized 15 July 1844

Ann CROSDALE d/o Rev. Henry CROSDALE & Mary Elizabeth CROSDALE born 21 March 1844 was baptized 18 July 1844

Mary Elizabeth CORBIN d/o John CORBIN & Maria CORBIN born 31 December 1843 was baptized 12 July 1844

Rosina Eleanor Spencer WHITE d/o Littleton L. WHITE & Mary Ann WHITE born 8 February 1844 was baptized 18 July 1844

Jeanette WHITE w/o Silas WHITE born 5 May 1821 was baptized 18 October 1844

Charles Edward WHITE infant s/o Silas WHITE & Jeannette WHITE was baptized 18 December 1844

Laura Ann WHITE d/o James WHITE & Adeline WHITE born 10 January 1845 was baptized 17 December 1844

Upshur JOHNSTON d/o William W. JOHNSTON & Rosina JOHNSTON born 7 January 1845 was baptized 14 January 1845

George Bozman WALLER infant s/o Washington WALLER & Mary Ann WALLER was baptized 17 March 1845

Gordon Handy McDANIEL s/o Marshall McDANIEL & Eliza McDANIEL born 1 February 1845 was baptized 17 March 1845

Eliza Ellen McDANIEL d/o Marshall McDANIEL & Eliza McDANIEL born 22 February 1837 was baptized 17 March 1845

Margaret Virginia McDANIEL d/o Marshall & Eliza McDANIEL born 27 November 1833 was baptized 17 March 1845

Emily Coulbourn DASHIELL d/o George W. DASHIELL & Virginia
DASHIELL born March 1845 was baptized 30 July 1845

Edward Hamilton HOLBROOK son of Samuel G. HOLBROOK & Maria
HOLBROOK born 25 May 1845 was baptized 19 October 1845

Rosina Elizabeth DAUGHERTY d/o John DAUGHERTY & Mary D.
DAUGHERTY born 13 October 1845 was baptized 20 October 1845

Sarah Elzey WATERS d/o William E. WATERS & Anna Maria WATERS
born 17 October 1844 was baptized 24 October 1845 and died
immediately afterwards.

Mary Eliza HYLAND & James Cash HYLAND children of James C.
HYLAND & Mary HYLAND were baptized 2 December 1845

James STANLEY s/o Rev. Harvey STANLEY & Mary Anne STANLEY
born 20 September 1845 was baptized 28 September 1845

John Gale HYLAND d/o Henry HYLAND & Hariett HYLAND born 28
July 1841 was baptized 1 January 1846
Virginia HYLAND d/o same born 13 January 1843 was baptized 1
January 1846
Ann Ayres HYLAND d/o same born 13 June 1845 was baptized 8
January 1846

George Arthur WOOLFORD s/o Levin WOOLFORD born 5 November
1841 was baptized 21 January 1846

Fanny Murray WHITE d/o Henry A. WHITE & Anne E. WHITE born
13 October 1843 was baptized 17 February 1846

William Murray Stone WHITE s/o Henry A. WHITE & Anne E.
WHITE born 15 September 1845 was baptized 17 February 1846
Bridget WALLER d/o William WALLER born 30 January 1845 was
baptized 11 April 1846

Anne Catherwood JONES d/o Catherwood JONES & Sally JONES
born 17 March 1846 was baptized 15 June 1846

Edward Reed WALLER s/o Robert WALLER & Marie WALLER born 3
February 1845 was baptized 19 November 1846

Edward White PARSONS s/o Rufus PARSONS & Charlotte PARSONS
born 24 April 1842 was baptized 30 November 1846
Roxanna Priscilla Handy PARSONS d/o same born 1 August 1844
was baptized 30 November 1846
Alice Anne PARSONS d/o same born 8 March 1846 was baptized
30 November 1846

Eliza Anna Wilmer WHITE d/o Levin WHITE & Eliza Ann WHITE
born 25 April 1845 was baptized 2 December 1846

Delia Margaret JONES d/o William H. JONES & Sarah JONES born
1 October 1846 was baptized 6 December 1846

Julia DASHIELL d/o George N. DASHIELL & Virginia Emily
DASHIELL born 9 July 1846 was baptized 7 October 1846

Samuel JOHNSTON d/o William W. JOHNSTON & Rosina M. JOHNSTON
born 9 March 1847 was baptized 17 March 1847

Ellen Polk WOOLFORD d/o John WOOLFORD & Ellen G. WOOLFORD
born 12 November 1845 was baptized 4 July 1847

Joseph Sidney McGRATH s/o Levin McGRATH was baptized 5
August 1847

Mary BELL d/o John H. BELL was baptized 4 September 1847

Eliza Jane PUSEY an adult, Samuel James Handy PUZEY s/o
William PUSEY, Sally Anne Broughton PUSEY d/o William PUSEY
and Eliza Jane PUSEY were baptized 23 January 1848

Francis Herbert WATERS s/o William E. WATERS & Anne WATERS
born 9 August 1847 was baptized 13 February 1848

Sarah Chathaime NICHOLSON d/o Rev. Joseph J. NICHOLSON &
Eliza NICHOLSON was baptized 11 March 1848

John Rufus DOUGHERTY s/o John DOUGHERTY & Mary G. H.
DOUGHERTY born 28 September 1848 was baptized on 6 October
1848

Carolina Polk BELL d/o John H. BELL & Mary BELL born 22
September 1848 was baptized 23 November 1848

Rosina Martin JOHNSTON was baptized 27 December 1848

Stephen Cecil DASHIELL d/o George W. DASHIELL and Virginia
DASHIELL born 3 July 1848 was baptized 27 December 1848

David Wallace WHITE d/o Levin WHITE born October 1847 was
baptized 9 May 1848

Robert James WALLER s/o Robert WALLER & Maria WALLER born
September 1848 was baptized 9 May 1848

Wilber Emerson McGRATH s/o Lewis McGRATH was baptized 9 May
1849

Tazwell JONES s/o Robert JONES of George JONES born 15
February 1849 was baptized 29 September 1849 and died.

Marietta BRITTINGHAM d/o William J. BRITTINGHAM age 1 yr, 10
months was baptized 2 November 1849

Laura Virginia BRITTINGHAM d/o William J. BRITTINGHAM was
baptized 2 November 1849

Henrietta Haynie JONES born 22 August 1840, Matthias JONES born 3 August 1842, Walter JONES born 29 December 1844, Mary Gale JONES born 2 December 1848 children of Alfred H. JONES & Henrietta JONES were baptized 2 November 1849

Edward Jerome NICHOLSON s/o Joseph J. NICHOLSON & Mary Eliza NICHOLSON born 3 December 1849 was baptized 12 March 1850

Patrick CAUSEY age about 45 was baptized 25 March 1850

Mary Irene MILES d/o Francis MILES born 21 October 1849 and was baptized 1 April 1850

William Howe FISHER s/o Nancy FISHER was baptized 13 April 1850 at the alms house.

James Cadmus BRINKLEY s/o Susan BRINKLEY was baptized on 13 April 1850 at the alms house.

Maria Louisa PARSONS d/o Rufus PARSONS age about 3 years was baptized 22 June 1850 being ill at the time.

Anna Irving HOLBROOK d/o Samuel G. HOLBROOK age 3 months was baptized 8 September 1850

Eliza Waters WOOLFORD d/o Levin WOOLFORD & Anna WOOLFORD, age 4 weeks and ill, was baptized 5 October 1850

Sarah Ellen Wailes DASHIELL d/o George W. DASHIELL age 11 months, was baptized 5 October 1850

Lawrence ROBERTS s/o Matthias ROBERTS & Cornelia ROBERTS, age 22 months was baptized 3 June 1849

Mary Evelen DOUGHERTY d/o John DOUGHERTY & Mary DOUGHERTY age 2 months was baptized on 2 December 1850

Ann Elizabeth WHITE d/o Silas WHITE, age 4 years was baptized 24 November 1850 at All Saints Church.

George Fox WHITE s/o Silas WHITE age 3 years was baptized 24 November 1850

Littleton Sydney WHEATLEY s/o Capt. Joseph WHEATLEY age 3 months was baptized 2 December 1850

Ellen Stewart BELL d/o John H. BELL was baptized 4 December 1850

Ellen Stewart JONES d/o Alfred H. JONES & Elizabeth K. JONES born 24 December 1850 was baptized 1 January 1851

Margaret Wilson JOHNSTON d/o William W. JOHNSTON & Rosina M. JOHNSTON born 7 February 1851 was baptized 16 February 1851

Henry Clinton ROBERTS son of Matthias & Cornelia ROBERTS born 18 Deember 1850 was baptized 15 June 1851

William Samuel MILES s/o William F. W. MILES & Caroline V. MILES born 18 March 1850 was baptized 1 June 1851

Susanna Waters STONE d/o Thomas W. STONE & Leah STONE born 24 June 1850 was baptized 5 August 1851

Augustus Whittingham CROCKETT s/o William B. CROCKETT & Anne D. CROCKETT born 4 January 1843 was baptized 22 August 1843

Eliza Rusam HYLAND born 17 January 1841, George Sydnham HYLAND born 30 September 1842 children of James C. HYLAND & Mary P. HYLAND were baptized 15 September 1843

Isabella KING d/o John H. KING & Charlotte KING born 1 May 1843 and was baptized 7 October 1843

John Henry SMULLING born 4 June 1839, George Washington SMULLING born 4 February 1841, Edmund SMULLING & Sarah SMULLING both born 25 April 1844 children of Nathaniel I. H. SMULLING & Elizabeth SMULLING were baptized 20 September 1843

Thomas Gillis WOOLFORD s/o John WOOLFORD & Ellen G. WOOLFORD born 25 October 1842 was baptized 25 September 1843

John WOOLFORD s/o John & Ellen G. WOOLFORD born 14 August 1838 was baptized 28 October 1838

Ann Maria BENNETT adult was baptized 24 September 1847

Arthur Woolford HOLBROOK s/o Samuel G. HOLBROOK & Maria HOLBROOK was baptized 19 December 1848

Thomas Morris WHITE s/o Silas WHITE & Jeanette WHITE born 28 July 1850 was baptized 18 June 1851

Mary Emily WHITE d/o Levin WHITE & Eliza A. WHITE born 28 July 1850 was baptized 18 June 1851

Caroline Virginia MILES d/o Parker DICKINSON & Eliza DICKINSON and wife of Francis MILES born 9 May 1830 was baptized 8 October 1851

Sydney Wilson LONG s/o Sydney C. LONG & Mary A. LONG born 17 October 1851 was baptized 17 January 1852

Roger WOOLFORD s/o Levin WOOLFORD & Anne E. WOOLFORD born 13 October 1851 was baptized 26 February 1852

Margaret Nichols ATKINSON d/o George S. ATKINSON & Elizabeth J. ATKINSON born 26 April 1852 was baptized May 1852

William Russum ATKINSON s/o Isaac S. & Susan H. ATKINSON born 5 March 1852 was baptized May 1852

Frederick Stanley WATERS s/o Dr. William E. WATERS & Ann M. WATERS born 22 August 1849 was baptized 18 August 1852

Nelson WATERS s/o Dr. William E. WATERS & Ann M. WATERS was baptized 18 August 1852

Anne Marie WALLER d/o Robert WALLER & Maria WALLER born 28 April 1851 was baptized 31 October 1851

John Bozman WALLER s/o Robert WALLER & Maria WALLER born 18 September 1852 was baptized 2 March 1853

Sarah Roberta Moore BAILY d/o Robert BAILY & Sally BAILY born 3 October 1852 was baptized on 9 March 1853

Juliana Elizabeth Handy BAILY born 27 March 1847, Matilda Frances BAILY born 18 February 1849, Amanda Jeanette BAILY born 19 December 1852 daughters of William A. BAILY & Susan W. BAILY were baptized 9 March 1853

Murray STONE s/o Dr. Thomas STONE was baptized 4 April 1853

Bell DASHIELL s/o George W. DASHIELL & Virginia DASHIELL was baptized 11 April 1853

Francis Howard ADAMS born 17 February 1849, Eugenia Brown ADAMS born 20 October 1845, Clotilda ADAMS born 24 February 1849 children John ADAMS (deceased) and Margaret ADAMS were baptized 16 April 1853

Olivia WHEATLY d/o Capt. Joseph WHEATLY born 10 March 1853 was baptized 20 April 1853

Elizabeth Collins BROWN d/o Leiut. John A. BROWN (USA) born 10 March 1853 was baptized 16 April 1853

Gibson CROSDALE s/o Edmund CROSDALE & Johanna CROSDALE was baptized 11 May 1853

William James BYRD born 26 April 1829 was baptized 5 June 1853

James Gillis HOLBROOK s/o Samuel G. HOLBROOK was baptized 5 June 1853

John Henshaw MOORE s/o Rev. James MOORE & Eliza Ann MOORE born 3 June 1853 was baptized 26 June 1853

Roberta Matilda James WATERS, Robert Eugene WATERS, Charles Clarence WATERS children of Robert C. J. WATERS & Matilda A. WATERS were baptized 22 July 1853

Joseph Frey ROBERTS s/o Matthias ROBERTS & Cornelia ROBERTS was baptized 24 July 1853

William King MILES s/o Alfred MILES & Arelia MILES was baptized 7 August 1853

Hoburt JOHNSTON s/o William W. JOHNSTON & Rosina M. JOHNSTON was baptized 7 August 1853

Elizabeth Bernard DENNIS d/o James U. DENNIS & Cecelia DENNIS was baptized 24 November 1853

John Francis MILES s/o Alfred MILES & Aurelia MILES was baptized 4 March 1854

William S. WATERS s/o William S. & Susan WATERS was baptized 18 April 1854

Ellen Stewart White HALL & Betsy HALL d's/o Lazarus HALL were baptized 22 May 1854

Julius Thomas DIX s/o Thomas DIX was baptized 18 June 1854

Joanna COLGAN d/o Joseph COLGAN was baptized 25 June 1854

Sarah Eliza BELL d/o John H. BELL was baptized 25 June 1854

John Trippe KING was baptized 2 July 1854

Tazwell JONES born 2 February 1849, Perry JONES born 7 June 1851, Lovenia Kate JONES born 6 March 1853 children of Robert JONES of George JONES and were baptized 22 July 1854

Thomas Henry Pennington COSTEN s/o James COSTEN was baptized 3 August 1854

Charlotte Emily BRITTINGHAM d/o William J. BRITTINGHAM was baptized 3 August 1854

Evelene Moore BRITTINGHAM d/o William J. BRITTINGHAM was baptized 3 August 1854

Julia Booth ATKINSON d/o Isaac S. ATKINSON & Susan H. ATKINSON was baptized 27 August 1854

Elizabeth Stewart JONES d/o Alfred H. JONES & Elizabeth K. JONES born 10 July 1853 was baptized 21 September 1854

Emily Virginia COULBOURNE d/o Stephen D. COULBOURN of Baltimore born 17 July 1854 was baptized 19 November 1854

Elizabeth Murray STONE d/o Dr. James STONE of Wicomico was baptized 18 January 1855

Ann Gillis STONE d/o Dr. James STONE was baptized 18 January

1855

Sidney WALLER s/o Robert WALLER & Maria WALLER born 28 March
1854 was baptized 20 January 1855

Henrietta Russum ATKINSON d/o Isaac S. ATKINSON & Susan H.
ATKINSON born 3 February 1855 was baptized 12 February 1855

Henry Wyatt Woodward MOORE s/o Rev. James MOORE & Eliza Ann
MOORE born 12 February 1855 was baptized 30 March 1855

Charles Henry DOREY was baptized 1 April 1855

Joseph Samuel COLGAN s/o John COLGAN was baptized 11 April
1855

Henry Herbert KING s/o Henry KING & Anne KING was baptized
23 April 1855

Samuel Handy WHEATLY s/o Capt. Joseph Wheatly born 8 April
1855 was baptized 11 May 1855

Eliza Ann KING d/o Dr. John Trippe KING & Sarah KING was
baptized 24 June 1855

Littleton Polk BELL s/o John BELL & Mary BELL was baptized
24 June 1855

Henry James WHITE s/o Henry WHITE was baptized 1 July 1855

Ida Mary Eliza HUGHES d/o Thomas HUGHES was baptized 17 June
1855 (mother burried the day before) sponsor Mrs. Sallie
JONES of Baltimore.

Lawrence ROBERTS s/o Matthias ROBERTS & Cornelia ROBERTS
born 21 March 1855 was baptized 23 July 1855

William James DIX s/o Thomas DIX born 1855 was baptized 30
July 1855

Charlotte Florence PARSONS d/o Rufus M. PARSONS & Charlotte
PARSONS was baptized 5 March 1856

Sarah Gillis DASHIELL d/o Dr. John W. DASHIELL & Eliza
DASHIELL was baptized 2 May 1856

Henry WHITE s/o Levin WHITE was baptized 11 May 1856

Sarah Esther DOUGHERTY d/o Robert DOUGHERTY was baptized 16
May 1856

Timothy Brian WHITE s/o Silas WHITE was baptized 18 May 1856

John Franklin LACATYS and Charles William Murray LACATYS
children of Charles LACATYS were baptized 19 October 1856

Aurelia MILES (sick) w/o Alfred MILES was baptized 18 February 1857, sponsors Mrs. John Miller & Mrs. Eliza A. MOORE

Addie Paulina WEBSTER d/o Gabriel WEBSTER & Ann WEBSTER born 17 November 1856 was baptized 2 April 1857

Elizabeth Greenwood WRIGHT d/o D. Wesley WRIGHT & Elizabeth. WRIGHT was baptized 5 May 1857

Hamden Polk DASHIELL s/o Alexander H. DASHIELL & Aurelia DASHIELL (deceased) was baptized 11 May 1857

Emily DIX d/o Thomas DIX was baptized 13 September 1857

Emma COVINGTON d/o the late Isaac COVINGTON was baptized 12 November 1857

John MORRIS s/o Henry E. L. MORRIS was baptized 21 April 1858

Rosina Upshur DENNIS d/o Dr. George R. DENNIS & Ellen DENNIS born April 1858 was baptized 5 May 1858

Elizabeth Elzey WOOLFORD d/o Col. Levin WOOLFORD & Annie WOOLFORD born 11 September 1857 was baptized 17 June 1858

James Booth ATKINSON, Henrietta Russum ATKINSON children of Isaac Atkinson & Susan ATKINSON were baptized 27 June 1858, sponsors William G. WOOLFORD & Virginia BOOTH.

Anna Rebecca BELL d/o John H. BELL & Mary Bell born 25 February 1857 was baptized 27 July 1858

Ella Bell Anna Maria DASHIELL d/o Dr. John H. DASHIELL & Eliza DASHIELL was baptized 6 September 1858

Franklin COVINGTON s/o Isaac COVINGTON deceased was baptized 6 August 1858

James Francis BRITTINGHAM, William Edgar BRITTINGHAM sons of William J. BRITTINGHAM & Henrietta BRITTINGHAM were baptized 20 August 1858

Sallie Adeliade DOUGHTERTY d/o Robert DOUGHERTY & Sallie DOUGHERTY was baptized 20 August 1858

Eva CHATHAM d/o H. Francis CHATHAM & Anne CHATHAM born 24 December 1856 was baptized 25 August 1858

Ida COSTEN d/o James W. COSTEN & Mary A. COSTEN born 3 February 1856 was baptized 7 September 1858

Susan Emily COSTEN d/o James W. COSTEN & Mary A. was born 4

February 1858 was baptized 7 September 1858

Sarah Alice TREHERN born 8 October 1850, Frederick James TREHERN born 2 September 1843 children of Gillie TREHERN (wife deceased) were baptized 13 September 1858. Sponsors Mr. and Mrs. Green, grandparents.

Candace Livia SUDLER w/o Joseph Sudler, an adult was baptized on 18 October 1858

Araminta Matilda HOLBROOK, adult w/o Thomas HOLBROOK was baptized 18 October 1858

Henrietta WOOD w/o James WOOD, adult was baptized 18 October 1858

Julia Matilda JONES d/o Mrs. Sallie JONES was baptized 18 October 1858

Sarah Frances COVINGTON d/o the late Isaac COVINGTON was baptized 18 October 1858

Jesse COVINGTON d/o the late Isaac COVINGTON was baptized 18 October 1858

James William COSTEN son in law of Mr. Martin was batpized 19 October 1858

George Tubman HARRIS an adult, s/o Mrs. John Fleming was baptized 17 November 1858

Joseph R. SMITH, an adult w/o Joseph SMITH Esq. was baptized 27 February 1859

Margaret Wilson MOORE d/o Rev. James MOORE & Eliza A. MOORE born 15 November 1858 was baptized 24 February 1859

John Hamilton BELL s/o John H. S. BELL & Mary W. BELL born 7 February 1860 was baptized 14 February 1860

Henry F. LOGAN born 20 March 1834 was baptized 5 May 1860

John W. C. WHEATLY s/o Joseph & Sarah L. WHEATLY born 4 October 1859 was baptized 5 May 1860

Selinia COGLIN d/o Joseph COGLIN & Catharine COGLIN born 14 October 1859 was baptized 17 July 1860

Eugenia WILSON d/o James WILSON & Jane WILSON born 25 April 1859 was baptized 22 August 1860

Maggie L. T. MILLS d/o Stephen MILLS & Angeline MILLS born 26 February 1859 was baptized 23 August 1860

Cornelia A. MILES d/o Matthias MILES & Caroline MILES born
30 November 1855 was baptized 27 August 1860

Robert Sidney MILES s/o Matthias MILES & Caroline MILES born
19 November 1859 was baptized 27 August 1860

George Davis ATKINSON s/o Isaac ATKINSON & Susan R. ATKINSON
born 23 March 1860 was baptized 2 September 1860 at Monie
Church

Carie HOLBROOK d/o Thomas HOLBROOK & Araminta HOLBROOK born
3 June 1860 was baptized 4 September 1860

Emily A. FRANCIS d/o Augustus F. FRANCIS & Sarah FRANCIS
born 9 June 1856 was baptized 4 September 1860

Minnie R. FRANCIS d/o Augustus F. FRANCIS & Sarah FRANCIS
born 31 December 1859 was baptized 4 September 1860

Matthias Jones SUDLER s/o Matthias SUDLER & Alphonsa F.
SUDLER born 29 May 1859 was baptized 6 September 1860

Elvary R. TAYLOR s/o Severn TAYLOR & Milky D. TAYLOR born in
the spring of 1860 was baptized 21 September 1860

Thomas R. STONE s/o Dr. Thomas STONE & Leah STONE born 1
September 1857 was baptized 223 September 1860 at Grace
Church

Horace Norman JONES s/o Alfred H. JONES & Elizabeth K. JONES
was baptized 28 September 1860

Margaret Ann OATS d/o George OATS & Susan OATS born 1 July
1859 was baptized 30 September 1860 at Monie Church

Joseph DASHIELL s/o James DASHIELL & Jane DASHIELL born 11
August 1860 was baptized 14 October 1860

Margaret Collins STEWART d/o Dr. William STEWART & Henrietta
STEWART born 9 October 1860 was baptized 22 October 1860

Samuel DIX s/o Thomas DIX & Josephine K. DIX born 18 July
1860 was baptized 20 January 1861

Virginia Stewart CROCKETT d/o Josiah CROCKETT & Sarah
CROCKETT born 12 November 1860 was baptized 6 March 1861

James Leander MORRIS s/o Henry MORRIS & Emily MORRIS born 21
January 1861 was baptized 22 March 1861

John William WALKER s/o John S. WALKER & Mary WALKER born 8
January 1861 was baptized 8 July 1861

Robert MILES s/o Alfred M. MILES & Virginia MILES born 23
October 1860 was baptized 12 July 1861

George Claud JONES s/o George JONES & Margaret JONES born 28 July 1858 was baptized 4 September 1861

Mary Wilson LONG d/o Sidney C. LONG & Mary LONG born 5 August 1861 was batpized 21 January 1862

Charles MAXWELL s/o Francis MAXWELL & Martha MAXWELL born 20 August 1861 was baptized 18 February 1862

Charles Tricket SMITH s/o William SMITH & Olivia SMITH born 30 November 1861 was baptized 14 March 1862

Sydney Long MADDUX s/o Edward MADDUX & Lydia MADDUX born 25 June 1854 was baptized 15 April 1862

Josephine MADDUX d/o Edward MADDUX & Lydia MADDUX born 30 October 1859 was baptized 15 April 1862

Arnold Elzey WATERS s/o L. L. WATERS & Lucretia WATERS born 9 October 1861 was baptized 19 April 1862

Richard DASHIELL d/o James F. DASHIELL & Jane DASHIELL born 13 October 1861 was baptized 19 April 1862

Lina WOOLFORD d/o Col. L. WOOLFORD & Annie WOOLFORD born 13 August 1861 was baptized 19 April 1862

Henry Lawrence BRITTINGHAM s/o William J. BRITTINGHAM & Henrietta BRITTINGHAM born 28 Oct ober 1859 was baptized 21 April 1862

Ellen Amanda BRITTINGHAM d/o William J. BRITTINGHAM & Henrietta BRITTINGHAM born 23 October 1861 was baptized 21 April 1862

Irving Waters McCLEMMY s/o George McCLEMMY & Martha McCLEMMY born 2 March 1862 was baptized 22 April 1862

Mary Ellen LARMOUR born 23 September 1855, George Addison LARMOUR born 23 March 1858, Lucy LARMOUR born 6 August 1861 children of John LARMOUR & Jane LARMOUN were baptized 24 April 1862

James Murray STONE s/o Dr. James STONE & Lucy STONE born 28 February 1860 was baptized 27 April 1762

Fanny STONE d/o Dr. James STONE & Lucy STONE born 3 June 1858 was baptized 27 April 1862

Eliza Russum ATKINSON d/o Isaac L. ATKINSON & Susan ATKINSON born 1 April 1862 was baptized 27 April 1862

James STEWART s/o Dr. William STEWART & Henrietta H. STEWART born 15 May 1862 was baptized 15 May 1862

32

William Gillis WOOLFORD s/o William Gillis & Williamanna
WOOLFORD born 3 May 1862 was baptized 25 June 1862

Harriet Etheline DASHIELL d/o Dr. Cadmus DASHIELL & Harriett
DASHIELL was baptized 4 July 1862

Mary Edith MILBOURN d/o Robert MILBOURN & Mary MILBOURN born
5 July 1862 was baptized 15 October 1862

Thomas HOLBROOK s/o Thomas W. HOLBROOK & Araminta HOLBROOK
born 12 July 1762 was baptized 20 January 1863

Isaac Dashiell JONES s/o Samuel B. JONES & Eglentine JONES
born July 1862 was baptized 5 March 1863

Esther Armstrong DASHIELL d/o James F. DASHIELL & Jennie
DASHIELL born 10 March 1863 was baptized 9 April 1863

Sarah Ann Mandusa Hatfield HORNER d/o John HORNER & Nancy
HORNER of Hungary Neck born 15 October 1860 was baptized 10
April 1863

John William Franklin HORNER s/o John HORNER & Nancy HORNER
born September 1862 was baptized 10 April 1863

Edgar James Lanison DASHIELL born 15 November 1855, William
Theodore DASHIELL born 19 October 1856, Cadmus DASHIELL born
17 September 1858, Fannie Louisa DASHIELL born 25 August
1860, Ann Cedonia DASHIELL born 5 February 1862, Gabriella
DASHIELL born 18 March 1853 children of Edgar DASHIELL &
Elizabeth Ann DASHIELL of Hungary Neck were baptized 10
April 1863

Alexander Denwood Lee JONES s/o Dr. Daniel JONES & Julia A.
JONES born 10 November 1859 was baptized 13 June 1863

George Lloyd BARTON s/o Rev. John BARTON & Ann Marie BARTON
born 30 May 1863 was baptized 19 June 1863

William Franklin NEWMAN s/o Sidney C. NEWMAN & Virginia E.
NEWMAN born 28 June 1862 was baptized 28 June 1863

Williamanna RENSHAW d/o Thaddeus W. RENSHAW & Alice RENSHAW
born 21 February 1862 was baptized 28 June 1863

William Yancy COSTEN d/o James COSTEN & Mary A. COSTEN born
13 April 1860 was baptized 28 June 1863

Jefferson Davis COSTEN s/o James COSTEN & Mary A. COSTEN
born 14 July 1862 was baptized 28 June 1863

Edward Pomeroy SUDLER s/o Joseph SUDLER & Candace L. SUDLER
born 3 April 1863 wasbaptized 15 July 1863 at Grace Church

James Francis COVINGTON s/o John E. COVINGTON & Mary E.

COVINGTON born 25 September 1861 was baptized 9 August 1863

Adrine WILSON born 23 April 1851, Samuel Marion WILSON born
17 April 1853, Ellen WILSON born 11 September 1854, Clara
Jane WILSON born 25 May 1863 children of James W. WILSON &
Jane WILSON were baptized 17 August 1763

Edwin Polk DASHIELL s/o Hampden H. DASHIELL & Elizabeth W.
DASHIELL born 23 Mary 1863 was baptized 1 November 1863

William Polk BELL s/o John H. BELL & Mary BELL was baptized
22 November 1863

Virginia Catherine MILLS d/o Stephen MILLS & Mary MILLS born
22 March 1863 was baptized 28 November 1863

Lucy Lee STONE d/o Dr. James STONE & Lucy STONE born 24
September 1863 was baptized 13 December 1863 at Grace Church

Ann Comfort LONG d/o Capt. Littleton LONG & Mary H. LONG
born 2 February 1863 was baptized 22 August 1863

John Hambleton LONG s/o Capt. Littleton LONG & Mary H. LONG
born 30 December 1863 was baptized 8 January 1864

Euphemia Ann WOOLFORD d/o William H. WOOLFORD & Williamanna
WOOFLORD born 9 January 1864 was baptized 5 May 1864

William Done STEWART s/o Lt. William STEWART & Henrietta H.
STEWART born 19 March 1864 was baptized 17 June 1864

Emily Rebecca WATERS d/o Levin L. WATERS & Lucretia WATERS
born 8 August 1863 was baptized 24 June 1864

Laura Griswold SUDLER d/o Joseph SUDLER & Candace SUDLER
born 9 July 1864 was baptized 22 July 1864

George Allen DASHIELL s/o James F. DASHIELL & Jane DASHIELL
born 9 March 1864 was baptized 12 July 1864

Henrietta BRITTINGHAM d/o William J. BRITTINGHAM & Henrietta
BRITTINGHAM born 30 January 1864 was baptized 18 August 1864

Maria Thomas POTTER born 21 January 1861, Susan Gunby POTTER
born 31 May 1863 daughters of Henry POTTER and Ann Maria
POTTER were baptized 11 September 1864

Jefferson Davis WEBSTER s/o Hamilton WEBSTER & Sarah WEBSTER
born 25 March 1864 was baptized 2 October 1864

Emily POLLITT born 20 August 1854, Calvin Henry POLLITT born
6 August 1859, Sidney POLLITT born 20 May 1857, Lewis
Jefferson POLLITT born 25 July 1861 children of Morris
Whittington POLLITT & Esther POLLITT were baptized 8
December 1864

William Gatherwood WALLER s/o W. Washington WALLER & Mary
Elen WALLER born 31 January 1865 was baptized 25 April 1865

Mary Jane BARBON d/o Soren BARBON & Elizabeth BARBON born 5
March 1864 was baptized 26 April 1865

Georgia WILLING, adult was baptized 28 June 1865

Emma Frances SMITH, adult was baptized 28 June 1865

Samuel Frank SMITH, adult was baptized 28 June 1865

Eleanor Elizabeth DASHIELL d/o Robert DASHIELL & Sallie E.
M. DASHIELL born 21 March 1865 was baptized 14 July 1865

Samuel Francis MILES s/o William F. W. MILES & Sallie E. S.
MILES born 18 June 1865 was baptized 26 July 1865

John Wesley COLGAN s/o John W. COLGAN & Sarah COLGAN born 17
May 1865 was baptized 19 August 1865

Norman Dashiell WANGEMAN s/o John C. WANGEMAN & Virginia
WANGEMAN was baptized 1 September 1865

Paul Jones MILES s/o Alfred M. MILES & Virginia MILES born
18 April 1864 was baptized 16 September 1865

Edward Page DUER s/o Edward F. DUER & Virginia W. DUER born
10 November 1864 was baptized 17 September 1865

Luther Williams PADEN born 19 January 1863, Malinda Frances
PADEN born 13 February 1865 chiildren of James PADEN & Mary
PADEN were baptized 24 September 1865

Sarah Jane ROSS d/o Levin ROSS & Elizabeth ROSS born 24 July
1863 was baptized 24 September 1865

Mary Amanda SMITH d/o Joseph F. SMITH & Mary E. SMITH age 4
years was baptized 22 October 1865

William Thomas Barton POWELL s/o Joshua Thomas POWELL &
Caroline POWELL born 17 October 1863 was baptized 29
November 1865

George Marion McCLEMMY s/o George F. McCLEMMY & Martha A.
McCLEMMY born 5 December 1864 was baptized 5 December 1864

James Washington COSTEN s/o James W. COSTEN & Mary A. COSTEN
born 19 March 1864 was baptized 29 December 1865

William Thomas Edwin RENSHAW s/o Thaddeus W. RENSHAW & Mary
E. RENSHAW born 30 January 1865 was baptized 19 December
1865

Elizabeth Warren CHATHAM d/o Frank CHATHAM & Elizabeth Ann

CHATHAM born 31 January 1863 was baptized 13 March 1866

Henrietta Maria Chaille WALLER d/o William Thomas WALLER & Mary Ellen WALLER born 3 January 1866 was baptized 22 May 1866

Alfred Jones STEWART s/o Dr. William STEWART & Henrietta H. STEWART born 25 January 1866 was baptized 13 July 1866

Susan Ingrham JONES d/o Edward A. JONES & Lucy JONES born 14 February 1866 was baptized 20 July 1866

Mrs. Ellen Gillis HOBDAY an adult was baptized 29 July 1866

Miss Mary Woolford HARVEY an adult was baptized 29 July 1866

Ellen Gillis HOBDAY d/o Joseph HOBDAY & Ellen Gillis HOBDAY born 15 March 1862 was baptized 29 July 1866

Mattie HOLBROOK d/o Thomas W. HOLBROOK & Araminta HOLBROOK was baptized 3 August 1866

Lavinia Ellen NEWMAN d/o Sydney C. NEWMAN & Virginia E. NEWMAN born 19 July 1864 was baptized 22 August 1866

George Washington NEWMAN s/o Sydney C. NEWMAN & Virginia E. NEWMAN born 13 January 186 was baptized 22 August 1866

Alice Florence PRICE d/o William A. PRICE & Ann Rebecca PRICE born 2 July 1862 was baptized 27 August 1866

Robert Ritchie MALONE s/o Sydney G. MALONE & Mary Ellen MALONE born 23 June 1866 was baptized 18 September 1866

Mary Barton STONE d/o Dr. James M. STONE & Lucy Stone was baptized 11 November 1866

Oliver Page BARTON s/o Rev. John A. BARTON & Annie M. BARTON born 25 September 1866 was baptized 21 November 1866

Julia Ethelinde Page CRISFIELD d/o Arthur CRISFIELD & Charlotte A. L. CRISFIELD born 1 April 1866 was baptized 5 January 1867

James Fairfax DASHIELL s/o James F. DASHIELL & Jane DASHIELL born 6 December 1866 was baptized 6 February 1867

Henry BRISCOE s/o Dr. Henry BRISCOE & Esther BRISCOE born 30 November 1866 was baptized 7 February 1867

Ann Eliza WHEATLY d/o Joseph WHEATLY & R. Priscilla WHEATLY born 30 November 1866 was baptized 17 February 1867

Minnie Evelyn MILLS d/o Stephen MILLS & Mary MILLS born 22 July 1866 was baptized 16 May 1847

William Edgar JONES s/o Daniel JONES & Julia A. JONES born 22 Ocober 1863 was baptized 10 July 1867

Laura Lee WHITE d/o Marcellus WHITE & Melissa WHITE born 27 March 1867 was baptized 10 July 1867

Laura Malinda BAKER d/o William BAKER & Mary BAKER born 15 November 1866 was baptized 10 July 1867

John Woolford DASHIELL s/o Hampden H. DASHIELL & Elizabeth W. DASHIELL born 18 November 1866 was baptized 4 August 1867

Bessie Gardner BRITTINGHAM d/o William J. BRITTINGHAM & Henrietta Gardner BRITTINGHAM born 28 September 1866 was baptized 4 October 1866

Theodore DashiellHOLBROOK s/o Thomas W. HOLBROOK & Araminta HOLBROOK born 17 February 1867 was baptized 18 October 1867

Sallie Franklin DASHIELL d/o Robert DASHIELL & Sallie DASHIELL born 15 June 1867 was baptized 30 October 1867

George Washington DIXON s/o John A. DIXON & Jennie A. DIXON born 17 April 1866 was baptized 2 January 1868

Winfield Scott TAYLOR s/o Sarah TAYLOR born 25 June 1866 was baptized 14 January 1868

William James Atkinson WHEATLY s/o Joseph WHEATLY & Rosa WHEATLY born 25 March 1865 was baptized 18 April 1868

Harry Murray STONE s/o Dr. Thomas W. STONE & Leah STONE was baptized 21 April 1868

George Barton WALLER s/o Washington W. WALLER & Maye Eleanor WALLER born 27 March 1868 was baptized 10 May 1868

Levin Littleton WATERS s/o Levin L. WATERS & Lucretia WATERS born 8 September 1866 was baptized 25 June 1868

Mary Anna WALLER d/o William T. WALLER & Mary Ellen WALLER born 25 July 1858 was baptized 25 July 1868

Florence Stone HARVEY an adult was baptized 16 August 1868

Grace HOBDAY d/o Joseph HOBDAY & Ellen Gillis HOBDAY was baptized 16 August 1868

George Barton FITZGERALD s/o Thomas A. FITZGERALD & Mary Ann FITZGERALD born 15 March 1868 was baptized 15 September 1868

Bruce White DUER s/o Edward F. DUER & Virginia W. DUER born 17 November 1866 was baptized 16 November 1868

Robert Ritchie CHATHAM s/o Francis CHATHAM & Elizabeth Ann

CHATHAM born 13 October 1865 was baptized 13 February 1869

Nettie May GARDNER d/o Grenville G. GARDNER & Sallie W. GARDNER was baptized 25 March 1869

Thomas Oliver NEWMAN s/o Sidney C. NEWMAN & Virginia E. NEWMAN born 31 March 1869 was baptized 6 April 1869

Louis DASHIELL s/o H. H. DASHIELL & Elizabeth DASHIELL born August 1868 was baptized 15 May 1869

Mary Louisa WALLER d/o James D. WALLER & Louisa WALLER born 5 September 1867 was baptized 11 July 1869

Cecelia WALLER d/o James D. WALLER & Louisa WALLER born 17 February 1869 was baptized 11 July 1869

Ellen Maria TYLER d/o George W. TYLER & Emily F. TYLER born 28 May 1869 was baptized 30 July 1869

Jannie BARTON d/o Rev. John O. BARTON & Annie M. BARTON born 22 July 1869 was baptized 31 October 1869

Henry Jackson WATERS s/o Levin L. WATERS & Lucretia WATERS was baptized 31 October 1869

John Woodland CRISFIELD s/o Arthur CRISFIELD & Charlotte A. CRISFIELD born 28 July 1868 was baptized 13 April 1870

Joseph Cottman BRISCOE s/o Dr. Henry BRISCOE & Esther H. BRISCOE born 9 February 1870 was baptized 10 February 1870

Minnie Mary Reid DASHIELL d/o Robert DASHIELL & Sallie E. M. DASHIELL born 24 September 1869 was baptized 9 June 1870

Rachel Done STEWART d/o Dr. William STEWART & Henrietta H. STEWART born 7 April 1870 was baptized 20 June 1870

Addie Henry BELL d/o John H. BELL & Mary BELL born 22 March 1870 was baptized 25 March 1870

William Jones WALLER s/o William Thomas WALLER & Mary Ellen WALLER born 19 January 1870 was baptized 3 April 1870

George Woodson JONES s/o Edward A. JONES & Lucy H. JONES was baptized 28 August 1870

William Henry DASHIELL s/o Hampden H. DASHIELL & Elizabeth W. DASHIELL born 19 October 1870 was baptized 4 December 1870

Archibald RENSHAW s/o Thaddeus W. RENSHAW & Mary E. RENSHAW born 25 March 1866 was baptized 1 March 1871

George Hitch RENSHAW s/o Thaddeus W. RENSHAW & Mary E.
RENSHAW born 4 Jun 1868 was baptized 1 March 1871

Emma Elizabeth Frances HORNER d/o Nancy HORNER born 24 June
1868 was baptized 8 March 1871

Charlotte Emma HORNER d/o Nancy HORNER born 24 June 1868 was
baptized 8 March 1871

Lillian Price NEWMAN d/o Sydney C. NEWMAN & Virginia E.
NEWMAN born 24 August 1870 was baptized 16 April 1871

Annie Duffield DOUGHERTY d/o H. H. DOUGHERTY & Annie
DOUGHERTY was baptized 19 May 1871

Annette WALLER d/o James D. WALLER & Louisa WALLER born 8
September 1870 was baptized 19 June 1871

Emily May SMITH d/o William H. SMITH & Olivia J. SMITH born
10 May 1871 was baptized 10 July 1871

Alice H. JAGGARD d/o Randall JAGGARD & Mary Jane JAGGARD
born 2 December 1871 was baptized 26 December 1871

James Anderson HICKMAN age 8 months was baptized 27 April
1872

Fannie Dashiell GREEN d/o James S. GREEN & Sallie A. GREEN
born 14 March 1864 was baptized 18 May 1872

Sarah Haddie GREEN d/o James S. GREEN & Sallie A. GREEN born
8 June 1867 was baptized 18 May 1872

Euphemia GREEN born 16 December 1864, John Robert GREEN born
30 July 1866, Alexander Hamilton GREEN born 25 November
1869, Gertrude Estelle GREEN born 10 April 1873, Mary ELiza
GREEN children of Alexander H. GREEN & Mary E. W. GREEN were
baptized 18 May 1872

Edwin Davis PUSEY s/o Edwin PUSEY & Catherine E. PUSEY born
6 January 1870 was baptized 22 May 1872

Eleanor Margaret PUSEY d/o Edwin PUSEY & Catherine E. PUSEY
born 24 December 1871 was baptized 22 May 1872

Mrs. Margaret Ann BANKS an adult was baptized 3 June 1872

Richard Irving SMITH an adult was baptized 2 June 1872

Eliza WATERS d/o Levin B. WATERS & Lucretia WATERS was
baptized 25 June 1872

John Barton YERBY s/o Lemuel YERBY & Sallie YERBY was
baptized 12 July 1872

Alice Gale STEWART d/o Dr. William STEWART & Henrietta H.
STEWART born 12 September 1871 was baptized 12 July 1872

Lucy Marshall WHITTINGTON d/o Joseph C. WHITTINGTON &
Virginia G. WHITTINGTON born 27 April 1872 was baptized 9
August 1872

Maggie May SLEMMONS d/o J. Edwin SLEMMONS & Anna Virginia
SLEMMONS born 13 June 1872 was baptized 27 August 1872

William Costen MILES s/o W. F. W. MILES & Sallie E. S. MILES
born 3 August 1869 was baptized 23 September 1872

Marion Laura MILES d/o W. F. W. MILES & Sallie E. S. MILES
born 7 August 1872 was baptized 23 September 1872

Arthur Gilbert Thomas DAVIS s/o Josiah DAVIS & Catherine M.
DAVIS of Dames Quarter born 9 July 1872 was baptized 25
September 1872

Elizabeth Scrivener WALLER d/o William Thomas WALLER & Mary
Ellen WALLER of Monie born 9 July 1872 was baptized 25
September 1872

Virginia Rose DUER d/o Edward F. DUER & Virginia W DUER born
23 August 1871 was baptized 29 September 1872

Lemuel BROOKS s/o Caleb BROOKS & Margaret Ann BROOKS was
baptized 27 October 1872

Annie Gillis HOLBROOK d/o Thomas W. HOLBROOK & Araminta
HOLBROOK was baptized 11 April 1873

Henrietta Isabelle DASHIELL d/o Robert & Sallie E. M.
DASHIELL born 6 December 1872 was baptized 10 July 1873

George Washington WALLER s/o James D. WALLER & Louisa WALLER
born 19 January 1872 was baptized 31 July 1873

Henry James BALLARD born 15 July 1867, Carrie Virginia
BALLARD born 21 July 1869, Richard Waters BALLARD born 19
November 1872 children of William R. BALLARD & Harriet
Elizabeth BALLARD were baptized 31 July 1873

Emma Franklin DOUGHERTY d/o H.H. DOUGHERTY & Annie DOUGHERTY
born 7 April 1867 was baptized 3 August 1873

Catherine Brodie ROBINSON d/o Albert K. ROBINSON & Catherine
E. ROBINSON born 8 April 1873 was baptized 24 August 1873

Joseph Benjamin REESE s/o William H. REESE & Elizabeth Ann
REESE born 23 May 1865 was baptized 27 August 1873

Louisa Annie HEARN born 18 July 1869, Jeanette HEARN born 29 October 1872, James Monroe HEARN born 20 February 1873 were baptized 9 October 1873

Martha Virginia Ann SCOTT d/o George W. SCOTT & Annie C. SCOTT of Dames Quarter was born 26 December 1871 was baptized 25 October 1873

Phillip Marcus SMITH an adult was baptized 3 November 1873 Sarah Lucy SMITH an adult was baptized 3 November 1873 Annie Cora SMITH an adult was baptized 3 November 1873

Samuel Kee STEWART s/o Dr. William STEWART & Henrietta H. STEWART was baptized 10 November 1873

James Upshur Dennis BRISCOE s/o Dr. Henry BRISCOE (deceased) and Esther B. BRISCOE was baptized 10 November 1873

Mattie Carey ROBINSON d/o Allen K. ROBINSON & Catherine R. ROBINSON was baptized 6 June 1874

Henry Lay DUER s/o Edward DUER & Vriginia W. DUER born 12 December 1873 was baptized 18 July 1874

Thomas Tyler BOULDIN s/o Thomas T. TYLER & Clara H. BOULDIN born 26 August 1874 was baptized 28 October 1874

Betty Ethelin LECATES an adult d/o Charles LECATES was baptized 29 January 1875

Caleb Thomas BROOKS an adult was baptized 29 January 1874

Harriett ROBERTSON d/o Henry H. ROBERTSON & Maggie E. ROBERTSON born 8 September 1874 was baptized 25 February 1875

Louisa DIXON d/o George W. DIXON & Emily C. DIXON was baptized 3 June 1875

Ernest COVINGTON s/o Scott COVINGTON & Ellen B. COVINGTON born 8 August 1875 was baptized 14 August 1875

Sarah Florence ELZEY d/o Jesse ELZEY & Caroline ELZEY born 28 December 1874 was baptized 4 October 1875

Betsy Ann Florence WATERS d/o Robert WATERS & Ellen WATERS born 6 October 1874 was baptized 4 October 1875

Cora May STEWART d/o Theodore STEWART & Margaret Ellen STEWART born 7 June 1875 was baptized 4 October 1875

Henry Silliman WALLER s/o William Thomas WALLER & mary Elllen WALLER born 17 July 1875 was baptized 12 October 1875

Lena Berry CURTIS d/o Levin H. CURTIS & Emma J. CURTIS born

18 July 1875 was baptized 18 November 1875

Joscph Woodland PUSEY s/o Samuel H. PUSEY & Biddy Ann PUSEY born 24 August 1875 was baptized 22 November 1875

Henry Jackson WHEATLY s/o Joseph WHEATLY Jr. & Rosa WHEATLY born 19 September 1875 was baptized 22 November 1875

Thomas Edgerton JONES s/o Berry T. I. B. JONES & Julia JONES of Rock Creek born 21 December 1875 was baptized 27 January 1876

Annie Jane SUDLER d/o Samuel S. SUDLER & Fannie M. SUDLER born 3 May 1875 was baptized 31 January 1876

Anna BALLARD d/o William B. BALLARD & Harriett Elizabeth BALLARD born 21 August 1874 was baptized 6 March 1876

Mary Magdalene MUIR d/o Thomas B. MUIR & Margaret MUIR born 16 February 1868 was baptized 9 March 1876

Lester James WALLER s/o James D. WALLER & Louisa WALLER born 165 May 1875 was baptized 9 March 1876

Marian Frances WALLER d/o Clarence C. WALLER & Ellen WALLER born 31 December 1875 was baptized 27 March 1876

Martha Anna LEWIS an adult d/o Minus LEWIS was baptized 2 April 1876

ELlen Gertrude BENNETT born 31 November 1870, Edward Reid Waller BENNETT born 20 October 1875 children of John T. & Virginia Emily BENNETT were baptized 2 April 1876

John Archibald PUSEY s/o Melvinia PUSEY born 23 Decebmer 1874 was baptized 2 April 1876

Henry James YOUNG s/o John Samuel YOUNG & Margaret YOUNG born 20 January 1863 was baptized 2 April 1876

Margaret Elizabeth YOUNG d/o John Samuel & Margaret YOUNG born 19 January 1866 was baptized 2 April 1876

Clarence Irving WHITE s/o Charles E. S. WHITE & Julianna WHITE born 1 May 1875 was baptized 20 April 1876

Margaret DIXON d/o Thomas DIXON & Laura Virginia DIXON was baptized 30 April 1876

Julia Edith YOUNG 6 years old, Edward Washignton YOUNG born 11 February 1875 children of John Samuel YOUNG & Margaret YOUNG were baptized 2 May 1876

Mary Isabella REESE d/o William H. REESE & Elizabeth Ann REESE born 7 July 1875 was baptized 15 June 1876

Jesse PUSEY s/o Edwin & Catherine E. PUSEY born 16 May 1876 was baptized 3 July 1876

Mary Done STEWART d/o Dr. William STEWART & Henrietta H. STEWART born 7 November 1871 was baptized 6 August 1876

Edward Carroll WATERS born 1 May 1873, Frances May WATERS born 7 October 1875, Richard Dale WATERS born February 1875 children of Herbert F. WATERS & Charlotte F. WATERS were baptized 6 September 1876

George William DASHIELL s/o Robert K. W. DASHIELL & Sallie E. M. DASHIELL born 5 April 1876 was baptized 2 October 1876

George William Thomas STEWART s/o Theodore F. STEWART & Margaret E. STEWART born 28 October 1876 was baptized 24 June 1877

Margaret Gertrude MUIR d/o William MUIR & Jane MUIR born 15 February 1876 was baptized 24 June 1877

Bessie Carey HAYDEN and Susie Markham HAYDEN twin daus/o Henry HAYDEN & Esther HAYDEN of Dames Quarter born 7 April 1877 were baptized 6 July 1877

Jamed Day SCOTT born 12 May 1874, Ednie Ida Earl SCOTT born 13 July 1876 children of George Washington SCOTT & Annie E. SCOTT were baptized 7 July 1877

Edith Lyle WALTON born 14 September 1876 d/o John WALTON & Kate M. WALTON was baptized 24 July 1877

Esther Rider DOUGHERTY d/o William Pitts DOUGHERTY & Mary W. DOUGHERTY born 20 January 1877 was baptized 25 July 1877

Lillie Catherine BARNETT born 26 October 1866, Thomas Lee BARNETT born 22 June 1868, John Stewart BARNETT born 10 October 1869, Paul BARNETT born 17 June 1871, Beatrice BARNETT born 17 August 1875 children of John W. BARNETT & Sarah J. BARNETT were baptized 12 August 1877

Ottis Barton GREEN born 18 February 1874, James Francis GREEN born 18 January 1876 children of Alexander H. GREEN & Mary E. W. GREEN were baptized 12 August 1877

George Ellen DIXON s/o George W. DIXON & Emily C. DIXON was baptized 4 November 1877

Annie Elzey WOOLFORD d/o Roger WOOLFORD & Clara WOOLFORD was baptized November 1877 in Annapolis

Walter James STEWART s/o Dr. William STEWART & Henrietta H. STEWART was baptized 12 August 1877

Levin Henry LLOYD born 1873, Addie Amanda LLOYD born 14

February 1875, Charles Granville LLOYD born 26 January 1877
children of George W. LLOYD & Annie E. LLOYD were baptized
12 August 1877

Mary Malinda MUIR d/o John MUIR & Virginia C. MUIR age 4
months was baptized 6 September 1878

Samuel Henry SUDLER s/o Samuel S. SUDLER & Fannie M. SUDLER
born 28 September 1877 was baptized 5 March 1878

George Waters JONES s/o Berry T. J. B. JONES & Julia JONES
of Rock Creek born 30 August 1877 was baptized 19 May 1878

Frank Harold COVINGTON s/o Scott COVINGTON & Ellen S.
COVINGTON born 20 January 1878 was baptized 19 June 1878

Mary Esther WILSON d/o Levin James WILSON & Mary Evelyn
WILSON born 12 February 1875 was baptized 9 January 1878

Bessie Carey HAYDEN d/o Henry HAYDEN & Esther HAYDEN of
Dames Quarter born 21 May 1878 was baptized 25 July 1878

John Henry POTTER s/o Mrs. Maria POTTER born 28 April 1766
was baptized 28 August 1878

William Barton POTTER s/o Mrs. Maria POTTER born 22 May 1868
was baptized 28 August 1878

Julia Atkinson WHEATLY d/o Joseph WHEATLY & Rosa WHEATLY was
baptized 19 August 1878 at All Saints Church.

Kate Rosalie PUSEY d/o Edwin PUSEY & Catherine PUSEY was
baptized 19 August 1878

Annie Eugenia GROSCUP d/o William H. GROSCUP & Susan A.
GROSCUP of Hengary neck born 4 September 1876 was baptized
11 September 1878

Vernetta Ann STEWART d/o Theodore F. STEWART & Margaret E.
STEWART born December 1877 was baptized 29 September 1878

Arula Avitha May MUIR d/o Miss Emily MUIR & Zadock TOWNSEND
illigitmate born 17 May 1878 was baptized 2 May 1880

Ida Zipporah MELSON d/o Matthias MELSON & Sarah MELSON born
27 October 1878 was baptized 2 May 1880

Jane Dougherty WILSON d/o Levin James WILSON & Mary Evelyn
WILSON was baptized 6 May 1880

William Price LAWSON s/o Patrick Henry LAWSON & Amelia M.
LAWSON was baptized 11 July 1880

Eliza Ellen Butler McDORMAN d/o George W. McDORMAN & Fannie
C. McDORMAN born 12 June 1880 was baptized 29 August 1880

George Bernard GROSCUP s/o William H. GROSCUP & Susan A.
GROSCUP born 12 September 1880 was baptized 14 November 1880

Mary Ellen STEWART d/o Theodore STEWART & Margaret Ellen
STEWART born 27 November 1879 was baptized 27 February 1881

Howard Stevens DUER s/o Edward F. DUER & Virginia DUER was
baptized 10 May 1881

Robert James STEWART s/o Theodore STEWART & Margaret STEWART
born 25 December 1880 was baptized 18 July 1881

Joseph Sidney ELLIOT s/o Sidney F. ELLIOT & Ellen ELLIOT
born 10 July 1881 was baptized 18 July 1881

John Barton HUMPHREYS s/o John W. HUMPRHEYS & Julia A.
HUMPHREYS born 27 November 1880 was baptized 20 August 1881

Alfred Walter GREEN s/o Alexander H. GREEN & Mary E. W.
GREEN born 12 September 1880 was baptized 11 September 1881

Ellen PRICE d/o James A. PRICE & Mary A. F. PRICE born 2 May
1881 was baptized 13 September 1881

Mary ELizabeth WHEATLY d/o Joseph WHEATLY & Rosa WHEATLY
born 16 May 1880 was baptized 25 September 1881

Blanch CHATHAM d/o Charles H. CHATHAM & Lou Ellen CHATHAM
born 5 July 1881 was baptized 2 October 1881

James Edward WILSON s/o Jevin James WILSON & Mary Evelyn
WILSON born 3 August 1881 was baptized 28 October 1881

Charlotte Haynie STEWART d/o Dr. William STEWART & Henrietta
STEWART born 23 July 1880 was baptized 3 October 1880

Henry Laurenson DASHIELL an adult was baptized 22 January
1882

William Thomas Gillis POLK an adult was baptized 22 January
1882

Esther PUSEY d/o Edwin PUSEY & Catherine PUSEY born 15
January 1882 was baptized 3 March 1882

Ellen May DIXON d/o Walter DIXON was baptized 5 June 1882
sponsor Mrs. Duer the grandmother.

William Morris WHITE s/o Thomas W. WHITE & Mary E. WHITE
born 15 October 1881 was baptized 10 July 1882

Lena Rigby WOOLFORD d/o Roger WOOLFORD & Clara WOOLFORD born
15 July 1882 was baptized 23 July 1882

Uriah James HEATH & Mary Emma HEATH children of James S.

HEATH & Alice HEATH born 1 October 1882 and were baptized 17
December 1882

Isaac Thomas LOKEY s/o William J. LOKEY & Sarah LOKEY born
25 January 1883 was baptized 28 January 1883

Edwin Morris OREM born 30 October 1871, Laura Ellen OREM
born 10 December 1873, Minnie Catherine OREM born 10
February 1875, Martha Jewell OREM born 16 November 1877,
Maud Seymour OREM born 26 July 1879, Daisey Keirgin OREM
born 26 April 1880 children of John K. OREM & Eliza A. OREM
were baptized 30 April 1883

Eliza Polk DASHIELL d/o Francis H. DASHIELL & Sallie J.
DASHIEll was baptized 17 June 1883

Lena PRICE d/o James A. PRICE & Mary A. F. PRICE was
baptized 2 July 1883

Myra Zenophone McCLEMMY born 31 August 1868, Robert Strattan
McCLEMMY born 4 April 1872, Louis Morris McCLEMMY born 7
February 1874, Thomas Elzey McCLEMMY born 10 April 1877,
Hough Gillis McCLEMMY born 8 July 1881 children of George T.
McCLEMMY & Martha A. McCLEMMY were baptized 30 August 1883

George Robertson DENNIS s/o William J. DENNIS born 23
December 1882 was baptized 9 December 1883

Mary Anna LANGFORD d/o Samuel H. LANGFORD & Nannie C.
LANGFORD born 7 December 1883 was baptized 11 May 1884

James Francis WILLIAMS s/o Thomas WILLIAMS & Maggie WILLIAMS
age 4 1/2 years was baptized 17 June 1884

Milka WILLIAMS d/o Thomas WILLIAMS & Maggie WILLIAMS age 5
months was baptized 17 June 1884

John Albert DOUGHERTY s/o George Albert DOUGHERTY born 8 May
1884 was baptized 19 June 1884

Elsie LAWSON d/o Patrick Henry LAWSON & Amelia M. LAWSON
born 14 December 1885 was baptized 22 July 1884

Ethelind LAWSON born 18 July 1882 d/o Patrick Henry LAWSON &
Amelia M. LAWSON was baptized 15 October 1884

Edward Franklin FITZGERALD d/o Thomas H. FITZGERALD Jr. &
Georgie Ellen FITZGERALD was baptized 27 July 1884

Ann Rebecca Price NOBLE d/o George W. NOBLE & Alice NOBLE
born 25 February 1884 was baptized 1 February 1885

Mollie Estelle LOKEY d/o Willliam J. LOKEY & Sarah E. LOKEY
born 25 August 1884 was baptized 8 February 1885

Charles Ashby HEATH s/o Charles HEATH & ALice Elizabeth
HEATH born 6 October 6 1884 was baptized 3 May 1885

Horace Cleveland HEATH s/o Thomas HEATH & Louisanna HEATH
born 4 November 1884 was baptized 10 May 1885

Elmore Lockwood HEATH s/o Robert HEATH & Mary HEATH born 25
October 1884 was baptized 10 May 1885

Elizabeth Matthews BROWN d/o John BROWN & Susan BROWN born
24 June 1881 was baptized 10 May 1885

George Walter ROBERTSON s/o Henry H. ROBERTSON & Margaret E.
ROBERTSON born 11 December 1878 was baptized 10 September
1885

Henry Hugh ROBERTSON s/o Henry H. ROBERTSON & Margaret E.
born 11 December 1878 was baptized 10 September 1885

Cecelia Hooe BRATTAN d/o Robert F. BRATTAN & Nellie H.
BRATTAN born 20 October 1885 was baptized 21 December 1885

Fannie White Stone SUDLER d/o Samuel S. SUDLER & Fannie M.
SUDLER born 1 May 1886 was baptized 29 June 1886

Elizabeth May DOUGHERTY d/o G. Albert DOUGHERTY & Emma E.
DOUGHERTY was baptized 1 July 1886

Patrick Henry LAWSON s/o Patrick H. & Amelia LAWSON born 24
March 1885 was baptized 17 October 1886

James Clifford PRICE s/o George H. PRICE & Mary PRICE born
28 August 1884 was baptized 17 October 1886

William Charles SEXTON s/o Patrick SEXTON & Victoria L.
SEXTON born 18 August 1882 was baptized 21 November 1886

Lucy Virginia BLOODSWORTH d/o Robert L. BLOODSWORTH & Laura
A. BLOODSWOTH born 28 September 1885 was baptized 26
November 1886

George Henry PALMATORY born 20 April 1827 d/o Robert
PALMATORY & Hannah PALMATORY, an adult was baptized 29
December 1886

Charles PACKARD age 40 years s/o Richard PACKARD & Ann
PACKARD was baptized 10 April 1887

Romeo DAVY born 24 April 1858, an adult s/o George DAVY &
Ann DAVY was baptized 10 April 1887

Daisy BELL POLK d/o George F. POLK & Malvina POLK born 14
November 1882 was baptized 17 April 1887

George Cleveland POLK s/o George F. & Malvina POLKborn 13

47

September 1886 was baptized 17 April 1887

Maude WILLIAMS d/o Thomas WILLIAMS & Maggie WILLIAMS born 28 August 1886 was baptized 17 April 1887

John Wesley CARROLL an adult was baptized 20 May 1887

Marion Heath SHOCKLEY s/o John A. SHOCKLEY & Mary A. SHOCKLEY born 12 May 1886 was baptized 20 May 1887

Nellie Drummond WOODSON d/o George W. WOODSON & Amanda J. WOODSON born 29 November 1886 was baptized 25 July 1887

Thomas Henry FITZGERALD s/o Thomas H. FITZGERALD Jr. & Georgie E. FITZGERALD born 15 June 1887 was baptized 21 August 1887

Sally Ann BROWN d/o John BROWN & Susan BROWN born 12 November 1883 was baptized 6 October 1887

Mollie BROWN d/o John BROWN & Susan BROWN born 18 June 1885 was baptized 6 October 1887

Eleanor Dennis BRATTEN d/o Robert F. BRATTEN & Eleanor H. BRATTEN born 13 July 1887 was baptized 14 November 1887

Ernest Hamilton WHITE born 5 April 1877, Julia Jannetta WHITE born 14 April 1880, Lulu Gertrude WHITE born 14 June 1884, Ethol Augusta WHITE born 18 August 1887 children of Charles E. S. WHITE & Julia A. WHITE of Monie Creek were baptized 8 March 1888

Mary Belle McGRATH born 8 October 1870, Louis Sidney McGRATH born 4 October 1879 children of Joseph S. McGRATH & Mary E. McGRATH were baptized 8 March 1888

Edward Franklin WALLER d/o Archer M. WALLER & N. E. WALLER born 4 December 1887 was baptized 18 March 1888

Druscilla Catherine McGRATH d/o Joseph S. McGRATH & Mary E. McGRATH born 31 May 1872 was baptized 25 March 1888

Virginia Margaret DIXON d/o N. Waller DIXON & Josephine DIXON born 10 June 1887 was baptized 21 April 1888

Lilly Regina HEATH d/o John W. HEATH & Susan HEATH born 13 March 1887 was baptized 21 April 1888

Sarah Priscilla STEWART d/o F. F. STEWART & M. E. STEWART born 11 July 1884 was baptized at Monie 14 May 1888

Sallie Jane WILLIAMS born 9 March 1884, Daisy Elizabeth WILLIAMS born 18 December 1887 daus/o Francis WILLIAMS & Laura WILLIAMS were baptized 14 May 1888

William Thomas YOUNG s/o John A. YOUNG & Rose Anna YOUNG born 25 December 1887 was baptized 14 May 1888

Robert Washington BLOODSWORTH s/o Robert L. BLOODSWORTH & Laura A. BLOODSWORTH born 26 March 1887 was baptized 14 May 1888

Ira Thomas HEATH s/o Thomas H. HEATH & S. F. HEATH born 5 January 1887 and baptized 18 May 1888

Caroline Elizabeth DISHAROON d/o Alex DISHAROON & Matilda C. DISHAROON born 28 August 1871 was baptized 24 June 1888 at Grace Church at Wicomico Point

George Fairfax REVELL born 20 October none, Mary May REVELL born 12 September none, Robert Washington REVELL, James Thomas REVELL born 1 June none, Fanny Florence Irving REVELL born 5 September none, children of Sidney F. REVELL & Mary Anne REVELL were baptized 20 July 1888

Archer Denwood ROSS s/o Charles ROSS & Nettie ROSS born 12 January 1888 was baptized 27 August 1888

Charles Edgar ROSS s/o William J. ROSS & Mary A. ROSS born 5 July 1888 was baptized 27 August 1888

Beulah Francis SHOCKLEY d/o John W. SHOCKLEY & M. A. G. SHOCKLEY born 26 November 1887 was baptized 27 August 1888 Lelia Edna HEATH d/o Charles W. HEATH & Letitia HEATH born 7 March 1884 was baptized at Monie 2 September 1888

Pauline HEATH born 8 February 1885, Ersula Hannah HEATH born 1 March 1886 daus/o Charles W. HEATH & Letitia HEATH were baptized 2 September 1888

Sidney Thomas WHEATLY s/o Samuel H. WHEATLY & Mary J. WHEATLY born 16 February 1886 was baptized 11 January 1889

Mary McIntyre HUMPHREYS d/o John W. HUMPHREYS & Julia HUMPHREYS born 11 February 1886 was baptized 9 march 1889

George Emily MESSICK s/o William B. MESSICK & Henrietta MESSICK born 20 June 1873 was baptized 31 March 1889 at Monie

Nathan James ANDERSON s/o William J. ANDERSON & Sarah H. ANDERSON born 22 December 1877 was baptized 31 March 1889 at Monie

William Benjamin ANDERSON s/o William J. & Sarah H. ANDERSON born 20 January 1874 was baptized 31 March 1889

Emily Estelle RIGGIN d/o George W. RIGGIN & Caroline J. RIGGIN born 14 September 1867 was baptized 3 April 1889

49

William Everly BROWN s/o Edward E. BROWN & Rebecca BROWN age 3 years was baptized 3 April 1889

John BROWN age 33 years was baptized 3 April 1889

Howard Waters WOODROW born 20 March 1880, George Stewart WOODROW born 22 December 1881, Elmer Pomroy WOODROW born 2 February 1888 sons of George W. & A. G. WOODROW were baptized 10 April 1889

Maggie SCHWARTZE d/o John F. SCHWARTZE & Maria SCHWARTZE born 23 May 1868 was baptized 11 April 1889

Mary Ida SHOCKLEY d/o William J. SHOCKLEY & Martha W. SHOCKLEY born 13 May 1877 was baptized 19 May 1889

Elizabeth Catherine REVELL d/o John H. REVELL & Dolly C. REVELL born September 1880 was baptized 12 July 1889

Henry Lawrence BRITTINGHAM s/o Henry S. BRITTINGHAM, & Maurilus BRITTINGHAM born 3 December 1888 was baptized 3 August 1889

Mary Estelle COVINGTON d/o James COVINGTON & Denise COVINGTON born 2 July 1889 was baptized 9 August 1889

Louisiana Frances HEATH d/o William MESSICK & Henrietta MESSICK born 23 January 1859,was baptized 15 November 1889

Susan BROWN d/o Jacob LAWSON & Charity LAWSON born 12 May 1851 an adult was baptized 8 September 1889

Irene Frances HEATH d/o Thomas HEATH & L. F. HEATH born 15 February 1889 was baptized 15 November 1889

Rufus Wilson LAYFIELD s/o Thomas W. LAYFIELD & Virginia LAYFIELD born 9 November 1882 was baptized 24 November 1889

Claude Harvey JONES s/o George C. JONES & Ella M. JONES born 13 March 1887 was baptized 29 December 1889

Nicholas Marryman JONES s/o George C. JONES & Ella M. JONES born 30 December 1886 was baptized 29 November 1889

Mark Lay COSTEN s/o H. T. P. COSTEN & A. L. COSTEN born 22 August 1889 was baptized 13 July 1890
Clyde Martin COSTEN s/o same born 25 July 1880 was baptized 13 July 1890

Henry Briscoe BOUNDS s/o H. J. E. BOUNDS & H. E. J. BOUNDS was baptized 13 July 1889

Jsoephine Briggs DAVY d/o Robert DAVY & Josephine born 6 May 1890 was baptized 3 August 1890

50

Maria Stone WALLER d/o W. G. T. WALLER & Lucy L. WALLER born 14 April 1890 was baptized 3 August 180 at Monie

Elmer Phillip COVINGTON s/o James COVINGTON & Annie COVINGTON born 5 August 1890 was baptized 5 August 1890

Clarence Wilson PHILLIPS s/o William J. PHILLIPS & Florence A. PHILLIPS born 1 November 1887 was baptized 19 October 1890

William Roger PHILLIPS s/o William J. & Florence A. PHILLIPS born 16 November 1889 was baptized 19 October 1890

Hattie Virginia PRICE d/o James A. PRICE & Mary PRICE born 14 August 1890 and baptized 25 November 1890

Annie Estelle LEWIS s/o John H. LEWIS & Mary M. LEWIS born 20 September 1890 was baptized 21 December 1890

Ella Pearl WALKER born 12 April 1884, Walter Lee WALKER born 9 August 1887, Paul Augustus WALKER born 18 October 1890 children of Theodore A. WALKER & Lenore WALKER were baptized 15 January 1891

Annie Virginia WHITE d/o Charles E. S. WHITE & Julia A. WHITE born 28 January 1889 was baptized 6 February 1891

Henry Martin HEATH s/o Thomas HEATH & L. F. HEATH born 20 January 1891 was baptized 11 February 1891

Samuel Ellis HEATH s/o Robert Wooley HEATH & Mary C. HEATH born 19 September 1890 was baptized 11 February 1891

John Mark MUIR s/o John E. MUIR & Maria MUIR born 13 November 1890 was baptized 11 February 1891

Mary Anna RIGGIN d/o George W. RIGGIN & Caroline J. RIGGIN born 13 January 1875 was baptized 19 April 1891

Lucy Gillis KELLEY d/o James P. KELLEY & Mary B. KELLEY born 4 March 1891 was baptized 12 May 1891 and died August 1892

John Kelley WEINBURGH s/o Richard K. WEINBURGH & Laura W. WEINBURGH born 10 November 1878 was baptized 31 May 1891

Annie Catharine WEINBURGH d/o Richard K. & Laura W. WEINBURGH born 15 February 1882 was baptized 31 May 1891

Bessie Wainwright WHEATLY d/o Thomas W. WHEATLY & G. E. WHEATLY born 18 December 1890 was baptized 7 JUly 1891

Ivy Pearl TWILLEY d/o George W. TWILLEY & F. TWILLEY born 9 April 1891 was baptized 12 July 1891 at Grace Church

Eleanor Louise LAWSON d/o P. H. LAWSON & Amelia LAWSON born

16 May 1891 was baptized 19 August 1891

Ramona RENSHAW d/o William T. RENSHAW & Lillie C. RENSHAW born 30 May 1891 was baptized 8 November 1891 at Grace Church, Wicomico Parish

William Stewart FITZGERALD s/o Charles W. FITZGERALD & Margaret FITZGERALD born 4 October 1891 was baptized 15 November 1891

Nellie Dennis JONES d/o Denwood JONES & Nellie R. JONES born 20 November 1891 was baptized 20 April 1892

Mary Edith WALKER d/o Theodore WALKER & Lenore WALKER born 1 May 1892 was baptized 1 August 1892 and died 12 August 1892

Helen Stewart TODD d/o William Harvey TODD & Ellen K. TODD born 28 September 1891 was baptized 18 August 1892

George Woodland DISHAROON s/o Samuel J. DISHAROON & Annie DISHAROON born 25 September 1891 was baptized 1 May 1892 at Monie.

Arthur FITZGERALD s/o Charles W. FITZGERALD & Margaret C. FITZGERALD born 25 January 1893 was baptized 2 February 1893

Robert Franklin BRATTEN s/o Robert F. BRATTEN & Nellie A. BRATTEN born 28 November 1892 was baptized 1 March 1893

William Polk BRITTINGHAM s/o H. S. BRITTINGHAM & M. A. BRITTINGHAM born 26 July 1892 was baptized 10 April 1893

John Henry BLOODSWORTH s/o Robert L. BLOODSWORTH & Laura A. BLOODSWORTH born 2 May 1892 was baptized 30 April 1893

Alice Martin BROWN s/o John BROWN & Susan S. BROWN born 9 August 1892 was baptized 18 June 1893

Gordon Somers YERBY s/o John Barton YERBY & Nellie E. YERBY born 25 October 1892 was baptized 25 June 1893 at Monie

Elsie PURNELL d/o Dr. John PURNELL & Carrie PURNELL born 10 Novembe4 1892 was baptized 25 June 1893

Emma Rebecca WINTER d/o Henry M. WINTER & Nettie J. WINTER born 15 January 1893 was baptized 23 July 1893

Martin Guy WALKER d/o Theodore A. WALKER & Lenora WALKER born 27 August 1893 was baptized 8 October 1893

William Washington WALLER d/o Archer M. & Nellie E. WALLER born 27 August 1893 was baptized 8 October 1893

Samuel James DISHAROON s/o Samuel J. DISHAROON & Annie E. DISHAROON born 28 June 1893 was baptized 29 October 1893

MARRIAGES

```
 4 Aug 1751 Whitty McCLEMMY to Sarah WATERS
29 Dec 1765 John COLLIER to Ann JONES
10 Feb 1760 Thomas IRVING to Sarah HANDY wid/o Samuel HANDY
10 Nov 1785 George IRVING s/o Thomas IRVING to Ann IRVING
            d/o John IRVING
28 Oct 1788 William WALLER of Monie to Bridget BOZMAN d/o
            George BOZMAN of Great Annamessex
28 Jan 1796 Matthew TRAVES to Priscilla HARRIS
18 Feb 1796 George DASHIELL to Molly JONES
23 Feb 1796 Thomas COLLINS to Hetty MALCOMB
 6 Mar 1796 Nicholas Evans MOORE to Nancy COLLIER
14 Apr 1796 John SMITH to Nelly McGRATH
 1 May 1796 Jesse COVINGTON to Nancy GATES
24 Apr 1796 Fairfax SMITH to Rebecca Enols WOBBLETON
23 Jun 1796 William HARRIS to Alice RENSCHER
 6 Jul 1796 Dr. John WOOLFORD to Ann Irving GILLIS
 6 Jul 1796 Parker BRERETON to Ann CHRISTOPHER
 7 Jul 1796 James MEZICK to Nelly COVINGTON
31 Aug 1796 Andrew McREADY to Sarah HOPKINS
   Sep 1796 Richard TULL to Betsy ONELY
14 Sep 1796 Dr. John KING to Harriett H. BELL
12 Oct 1796 Isaiah HAYMAN to Peggy Renscher POLLITT
13 Oct 1796 John CARTER to Hetty MATTHEWS
17 Nov 1796 Robert FOWLER to Sarah FOWLER
17 Nov 1796 Nicholas TULL to Nelly CHENEY
22 Dec 1796 Moses DUNN to Mary MEZICK
11 Jan 1797 Lazarus COTTMAN to Betsy BISHOP
12 Jan 1797 Francis ROSS to Nancy LONG
25 Jan 1797 Isaac HARRIS to Margaret TAYLOR
25 Jan 1797 Zadock MITCHELL to Sarah VENABLES
26 Jan 1797 Andrew ADAMS to Mary Taylor
 2 Feb 1797 John KELLY to Sarah WHITE
 4 Feb 1797 Thomas HERON to Polly ABBOTT
16 Feb 1797 John McGRATH to Ann SMITH
22 Feb 1797 Daniel MEZICK to Priscila WINRIGHT
23 Feb 1797 Henry DASHIELL to Jane COTTINGHAM
23 Feb 1797 John HITCH to Amelia DISHAROON
30 Mar 1797 Planner PUSEY to Sarah HAYMAN
 9 Apr 1797 Michael MURRAY to Polly SIMS
27 Apr 1797 Robert COLLIER to Sarah RITCHIE
17 May 1797 John WHITTINGHAM ADAMS to Sally DISHAROON
19 May 1797 George PARSONS to Priscilla DISHAROON
15 Jun 1797 William WALLER to Priscilla WALLER
 6 Jul 1797 Henry JONES to Elizabeth JONES
30 Jul 1797 James GLASGOW to Elizabeth REVEL
 6 Aug 1797 Benjamin SMITH to Sarah Ann NEWMAN
17 Aug 1797 William TAYLER to Priscilla FURNISS
 7 Sep 1797 John JONES to Sarah MOORE
14 Sep 1797 Eli VINSON to Comfort ADAMS
 8 Oct 1797 William JONES to Sally LAWS
18 Oct 1797 Shiles CROCKETT to Elizabeth DALTRIEN
19 Oct 1797 John WROTTEN to Catherine DARBY
25 Oct 1797 William BERKHEAD to Sally WEATHERLY
```

```
 9 Nov 1797 John HOPKINS to Leah DICKINSON
20 Nov 1797 Hugh PORTER to Peggy WINRIGHT
30 Nov 1797 Thomas CURTIS to Peggy BLOODSWORTH
14 Dec 1797 John TAYLER to Temperance ACKWORTH
14 Dec 1797 Benjamin WALLER to Mary ADAMS
17 Dec 1797 Isaac R. AUSTIN to Martha G. MALCOMB
18 Dec 1797 Esme WALLER to Sally ELZEY
20 Dec 1797 Covington CORDERY to Ann WINRIGHT
21 Dec 1797 Thomas JONES to Priscilla DUNN
24 Jan 1798 Isaac HOPKINS to Martha HARRIS
25 Jan 1798 George KIBBLE to Rosetta COLLINS
25 Jan 1798 Thomas WHITE to Ann WRIGHT
29 Jan 1798 William ROBERTS to Sarah RENSCHER
11 Feb 1798 James U. WEST to Sarah NICHOLSEN
12 Feb 1798 Henry LANGSDALE to Elizabeth PORTER
22 Feb 1798 Richard BENNETT to Sally TULLY
 1 Mar 1798 Elzey HARRIS to Mary KNIGHT
21 Mar 1798 Joseph HARDY to Mary Ann WALLER
20 May 1798 Richard DUNN to Mary LARAMOUR
22 May 1798 Thomas GOSLEE to Nancy DENWOOD
17 Jun 1798 Richard K. HANDY to Betsy GORDON
20 Jun 1798 Richard WATERS to Mary Day CHENEY
 8 Jul 1798 James WINGATE to Alice MARTIN
18 Jul 1798 James HARRIS to Mary R. HOBBS
29 Jul 1798 William SLAYTON to Rebecca WRIGHT
12 Aug 1798 Moses DUNN to Sukey JONES
 8 Sep 1798 William BOUNDS to Peggy WAILES
26 Sep 1798 Zadock Green to Ellenor HOLDER
26 Sep 1798 George DASHIELL to Sarah WILSON
30 Sep 1798 Thomas VINCENT to Sally TAYLOR
11 Oct 1798 James GIBSON to Nancy MERRIDAY
24 Oct 1798 Samuel HOLBROOK to Nelly D. GILLIS
26 Dec 1798 Charles DIGNER to Polly CLARK
27 Dec 1798 William WHITE to Ann DONE
 3 Jan 1799 John MILYKIN to Sally STEVENS
15 Jan 1799 Thomas GILES to Betsy LEATHERBURY
21 Jan 1799 David WHITNEY to Rachel EVANS
22 Jan 1799 Stephen THORNS to Sally OWENS
24 Jan 1799 Levin BOTHAM to Ann WHAYLAND
31 Jan 1799 John REVEL to Sally ABBOTT
19 Mar 1799 Matthias HOPKINS TO Nelly DASHIELL
20 Mar 1799 Gowan WHITE to Biddy HICKMAN
29 Mar 1799 William Gillis WATERS to Ann Glasgo ELZEY
 4 Aug 1800 John VILLORY to Mary JONES
 9 Nov 1800 John CAMPBELL to Betsy RONAN
13 Nov 1800 Zorobable MUNGAR to Peggy MARTIN
·11 Dec 1800 William H. LANKFORD to Lydia HAYMAN
 8 Jan 1801 Zachariah CHAILLE to Hessy MATTHEWS
15 Jan 1801 Thomas LAWES to Nelly LONG
28 Jan 1801 Hezekiah DORMAN to Amelia HAYMAN
26 Mar 1801 James KELLY to Katy JONES
 4 Apr 1801 Israel PANTER to Sarah LONG
30 Apr 1801 Michael MURRAY to Nancy MADDUX
12 May 1801 William AUSTIN to Milly CLARK
 3 Jun 1801 Jesse HUGHES to Sarah Harmonson WATERS
```

```
 4 Jun 1801 Thomas WALSTON to Leah WHITE
10 Aug 1801 Thomas KING to Mary MALCOLM
 2 Sep 1801 George SHIPHAM to Polly HALL
 8 Sep 1801 Samuel ADAMS to Nancy WHITTINGHAM
10 Nov 1801 Jesse ELLIOTT to Elizabeth JONES
30 Jan 1811 Elisha WHITELOCK to Susanna C. ADAMS
18 Dec 1818 Samuel LEATHERBURY to Mary DONE
28 Jan 1818 Thomas MARTIN to Ann HILL
11 Feb 1818 Risdon BLOODSWORTH to Susan KIRWIN
26 May 1818 Lewis McDORMAN to Nancy AIKMAN
17 Jun 1818 William WALLER Jr. to Bridget D. JONES
13 Aug 1818 David LONG of Kentucky to Henrietta ELZEY
 8 Sep 1818 Levin LEATHERBURY to Elizabeth LEATHERBURY
14 Sep 1818 John SPENCE to Leah Handy GUY
 1 Oct 1818 John J. JAMES to Sally P. DONE
27 Oct 1818 John DUFFEE to Elizabeth CANTWELL
 9 Nov 1818 Thomas SKINNER to Eleanor B. RENCHER
18 Mar 1826 Joseph SUDLER to Henrietta JONES
25 Apr 1826 Rev. William JONES to Julianna HOLBROOK
 5 May 1826 William BOZMAN to Charity MILLIGAN
 6 Dec 1826 Edward S. SNEAD to Susan W. DENNIS
10 Jan 1827 Littleton S. WHITE to Mary Ann JONES
30 May 1827 Levin G. WATERS to Eliza R. W. HYLAND
 1 Jul 1827 William POLLITT to Elizabeth H. HYLAND
 7 Nov 1825 John H. KING to Sally E. G. C. CROCKETT
 5 May 1825 Isaac REVELL to Nancy GIBBONS
 6 Aug 1828 Dr. John KING to Ann D _____
24 Sep 1828 Thomas G. BEAUCHAMP to Leah W. KING
 2 Apr 1835 John W. REDDEN to Sarah Ann M. HAYMAN
27 Aug 1835 A. CHRISTOPHER to Amelia HOPKINS
20 Apr 1836 Andrew K. SANDERS to Amanda E. DASHIELL
 1 Nov 1837 John WOOLFORD to Ellen G. POLK
15 Mar 1838 Levin PARKER to Susan BEAUCHAMP
18 Feb 1839 George DRURA to Margaret R. LONG
16 Apr 1839 John H. STEWART to Mary G. JONES
23 Apr 1839 William G. WOOLFORD to Matilda E. HOLBROOK
 8 Sep 1841 Stephen COLBOURN to Emily DASHIELL
22 Sep 1842 John C. HORSEY to Eleanor NEWMAN
22 Dec 1842 William BELL to Amanda E. SANDERS
 8 Feb 1843 John DOUGHERTY to Mary D. H. BOWLAND
22 Feb 1843 John H. DENNIS to Henrietta A. LONG
31 Oct 1843 Robert J. WALLER to Maria PARSONS
 7 Aug 1844 Samuel G. HOLBROOK to Maria WOOLFORD
 6 May 1846 William A. BAILEY to Susan W. COVINGTON
20 Jul 1846 Robert PATERSON to Eliza WHITE
 1 Aug 1846 Isaac W. PARKER of Kentucky to Mary Jane
            STEWART, deaf & dumb
 3 Oct 1846 H. BELL to Mary W. POLK
 6 Jan 1847 William J. BRITTINGHAM to Henrietta C. LAWRENCE
16 Feb 1847 Robert BAILEY to Sally A. COVINGTON
16 Mar 1847 Eli J. VINCENT of Cincinnatti Ohio to Elizabeth
            Ellen DISHAROON of Somerset County
16 Jun 1847 Benjamin I. DASHIELL to Leah Matilda STEWART
16 Dec 1847 Alfred Henry JONES to Elizabeth Ker STEWART
19 Jan 1848 William J. THOMPSON of Dorcester County to Emily
```

```
                Frances WATERS d/o R. C. B. WATERS
14 Jul 1849 Sydney C. LONG to Mary Ann S. WILSON
30 Apr 1849 Dr. James M. STONE to Lucinda Gillis JONES
 9 Oct 1849 Major L. W. WOOLFORD to Anne E. WATERS
 3 Sep 1849 Zadock MADDUX to Jane JONES
 3 Sep 1849 Littleton Henry MADDUX to Henrietta Susan
                STEWART
19 Dec 1849 George Ballard R. WALLER to Isabella M. WHITE
29 Dec 1849 William MITCHELL & Elizabeth BOOTH both of
                Salisbury, in the jail of Somerset County
29 Jan 1850 A. A. PACKARD of Massachusetts to Elizabeth
                JONES d/o Robert JONES of George JONES
 5 May 1850 Fielder AUSTIN to Mary Jane COLLIER

30 Apr 1851 George S. ATKINSON to Elizabeth JONES
29 Nov 1859 Dr. William STEWART to Henrietta H. JONES
 6 Dec 1859 Levin L. WATERS to Lucretia JONES
15 Aug 1860 John H. REVELL to Dolly C. WILLING
 5 Dec 1850 John E. COVINGTON to Mary E. LANKFORD
 9 Jan 1861 George WHEATLY to Emily MEZICK at Monie
 1 Apr 1861 Robert H. MILBOURN to Mary E. WILKINS
 3 Sep 1861 Sidney C. NEWMAN to  Virginia E. PRICE at Monie
24 Apr 1862 Christian WANGAMAN to Virginia K. DASHIELL
 8 Jan 1863 Joshua T. POWELL to Mrs. Caroline MILES
29 Jan 1863 William Edgar JONES to Maria E. M. REID
29 Jan 1863 George S. DASHIELL to Mary E. ROSS of Hungary
                Neck
 1 Feb 1863 Thomas H. TANKERSLY to Laura C. WEBSTER
 2 Apr 1863 Sorin BARBON to Elizabeth HITCH
10 Apr 1863 Alexander THOMAS to Harriett HORNER at Hungary
                NECK
25 Jun 1863 James S. GREEN to Sallie A. BAILEY at Grace
                Church, Wicomico Parish
15 Oct 1863 George HAYWARD to Anne CROSDALE
 5 Nov 1863 Edward J. BOWER to Julia M. JONES
15 Dec 1863 J. Francis A. TULL to Esther A. WILSON
13 Jan 1864 Alexander H. GREEN to Mary E. W. BAILEY at Grace
                Church
28 Jan 1864 Edward G. DUER to Virginia W. DIXON
 3 Feb 1864 William Thomas WALLER to Mary Ellen WALLER at
                at the house of George B. WALLER of Monie
17 Mar 1864 Thaddeus W. RENSHAW to Mary E. BOUNDS at Grace
                Church
28 Apr 1864 Robert DASHIELL to Sallie E. M. WALLER at house
                of George B. WALLER of Monie
 7 Mar 1865 Jacob MISTER to Virginia WILSON at the
                Washington Hotel, Princess Anne.
25 Mar 1865 William R. BALLARD to Harriett Elizabeth HYLAND
                at Dr. Hyland's in  St. Peters Creek
 4 May 1865 Thomas H. HOLLAND to Mary E. HASTINGS
27 Jul 1865 William J. BRITTINGHAM to Henrietta S. GARDNER
11 Oct 1865 Henry BRISCOE to Esther H. COTTMAN at
                "Motherton"
26 Oct 1865 Joseph WHEATLY to Rosa ROSS
29 Nov 1865 Samuel J. TAYLOR to Amanda F. PUSEY
```

```
24 Jan 1866 William BAKER to Mary SHORES
16 May 1866 Josiah DAVIS to Catherine M. HAYDEN
 6 Jun 1866 George W. TYLER to Emily F. PRICE at Monie
13 Jun 1866 Humphreys SHORES to Elizabeth POLK
19 Jun 1866 William V. HOGE to Virginia L. HYLAND at Mrs.
            Harriet HYLAND house St. Peters Creek
25 Jun 1866 George W. STRADELEY to Sarah WARD
22 Nov 1866 Dr. John D. SCOTT Sr. to Julia F. WHITE at Monie
21 Jan 1867 William J. ANDERSON to Sarah H. LANGFORD at
            house of Nathan J. LANGFORD
 7 Feb 1867 Gustavous W. WHITE to Laura RIALL at Tyaskin
 4 May 1867 John H. GREEN & Eliza E. BROWN at Somerset Hotel
19 Jun 1867 Asa A. TURNER to Elizabeth A. FORMAN at Goose
            Creek
11 Jul 1867 John T. BENNETT to Virginia Emily JONES at house
            of Daniel W. JONES
11 Sep 1867 John H. BRILEY to Anne R. JONES at Spring Hill
30 Oct 1867 Edward FORD to Eliza WHITE at Dames Quarter
 5 Dec 1867 Grenville G. GARDNER to Sallie W. DASHIELL
20 Feb 1868 Robert H. MUIR to Louisa OATS
 7 May 1868 Levin W. LLOYD to Susanna W. FLOWERS
 8 Sep 1868 Francis W. MILBOURN to Leah E. ELLIS
17 Jun 1869 J. Edwin SLEMMONS to Annie Virginia MORRIS at
            Workington
 8 Jun 1870 William E. CANTWELL to Mary E. MADDUX
15 Jun 1870 Levin P. WHITE to Indianna WALLACE at Monie
 3 Jul 1870 James H. BUSSELS to Laura H. WHITE
17 Aug 1870 Lawson J. MASON to Emma J. PARKS at Grace Church
18 Aug 1870 Hon. T. Lyle DICKEY to Mrs. Beula C. HURST
 3 Mar 1871 Henry BULEMAN to Mary E. HORNER, Hungary Neck
 8 Mar 1871 Revill P. SIMMS to Sarah E. MASON, Hungary Neck
 9 Mar 1871 George W. SCOTT to Annie C. McDORMAN
 6 Jul 1871 William R. T. PITTS to Mary Ella DIXON at house
            of Thomas J. DIXON Esq.
16 Aug 1871 Isaac G. BALLARD to Mary LONG
18 Jan 1872 Edgar W. McMASTER to Isabella C. FLEMING
31 Aug 1872 Patrick SEXTON to Victoria JONES
13 Jun 1870 Jacob R. JONES to Susan M. BLOODSWORTH
21 May 1873 William Pitt DOUGHERTY to Mary W. RIDER
 2 Jun 1873 George W. RIDER to Melissa JONES
 9 Jul 1873 Thomas D. GILES to Lucy HEARN
 9 Dec 1873 Henry H. ROBERTSON to Margaret E. DASHIELL
 8 Apr 1874 George W. DIXON to Emily Charlotte BRITTINGHAM
23 Apr 1874 Berry T. J. B. JONES to Julia BAILY at residence
            of father William BAILY
24 Jun 1874 Samuel S. SUDLER to Fannie M. WHITE at "Hansel"
            on the Manokin
28 Sep 1874 Samuel H. PUSEY to Biddy Ann WHEATLY at house of
            father Joseph WHEATLY
15 Oct 1874 Robert H. HOOPER to Susan UPSHUR at Fairmount
15 Oct 1874 Scott COVINGTON to Ellen Stewart BELL
 2 Dec 1874 Thomas DIXON to Laura Virginia BRITTINGHAM
29 Dec 1874 Benjamin LANGFORD to Mrs. Mary DOUGHERTY
 3 Feb 1875 Clarence C. WALLER to Ellen WILSON at Crisfield
10 Feb 1875 William J. MUIR to Eunice Jane DENNIS at Monie
```

```
 7 Sep 1875 Thomas P. WALTON to Laura H. JONES
19 Oct 1875 Charles P. CRAIG to Irene DASHEILL at house of
            H.H. DASHIELL
19 Oct 1875 William J. LOKEY to Sarah HEATH at Monie
 9 Dec 1875 John WALTON to Kate M. JONES
11 Dec 1875 James T. ROBINSON to Anna McGRATH
23 Mar 1876 George W. JONES to Emily Virginia BLOODSWORTH at
            home of Robert BLOODSWORTH on Monie
18 Aug 1876 Nathan EMMENIGER to Emma Cornelia DOUGHERTY
 1 Nov 1876 John T. WHITE to Willie A. PARKS
12 Dec 1876 George A. BOZMAN to Sallie E. NUTTER, St.Peters
27 Dec 1876 Richard Irving SMITH to Annie F. CHATHAM
28 Dec 1876 Sidney REVIL to Annie HEATH
17 Jan 1877 Levin James WILSON to Mary Evelyn DOUGHERTY
            Lower Trappe
23 May 1877 Timothy J. ADAMS to Matilda F. BAILY
12 Sep 1877 Francis McDORMAN to Ida MARSHALL  Dames Quarter
17 Dec 1877 John E. PARKS to Amanda E. PARKS
15 Mar 1878 John W. HUMPHREYS to Julia A. McINTYRE  Grace
            Church
28 Maar 1878 Matthew DONNOCK to Sarah William BOUNDS
 7 Jan 1879 James E. KELLY to EMily Florence WILLING
 8 Jan 1879 John W. CARROLL to Mary Jane DAVY at Fairmount
25 Mar 1879 George W. WOODROW to Amanda Jeanette BAILY
30 Jul 1879 Patrick Henry LAWSON to Amelia Maria PRICE at
            Little Monie
24 Jun 1879 Thomas m. WHITE to Mary E. PRICE at Monie
17 Sep 1879 George B. WALLER to Lovy A. JONES at Grace Ch.
 6 Oct 1879 William A. PRICE to Henrietta PHOEBUS at
            "Colbrook"
21 Jul 1880 James Aldophus PRICE to Mary A. F. BRADSHAW at
            Annamessex
 8 Sep 1880 John F. WEBSTER to Lucy CONDIFF
30 Nov 1880 Francis H. DASHIELL to Sallie Gillis DASHIELL
 5 Jan 1881 B. WALTON to Clara S. PENNOCK at "WOODHILL"
 3 Feb 1881 Joseph Edward TRADER to Lucretia HARRIS
22 Mar 1881 John E. MUIR to Maria Thomas POTTER
 9 Feb 1882 George H. WAPLES to Mary H. CONNER
25 May 1882 Samuel H. LANGFORD to Mamie C. JONES
30 Jul 1882 Robert H. HORNBY to Florence E. WILLING
 6 Sep 1882 Archie M. WALLER to Eleanor Elizabeth Ann
            DASHIELL at home of Robert DASHEILL in Monie
21 Dec 1882 George W. MADDOX to Sallie Y. SUDLER in
            Fairmount
26 Dec 1882 Washington BEAUCHAMP to Mary E. HORSEY near
            Marion
 2 Jan 1883 George W. NOBLE to Alice Florence PRICE on
            Little Monie
17 Jan 1883 Thomas H. FITZGERALD Jr. to Georgie Ellen WALLER
            at Monie
 2 Jun 1883 Bates L. CRIST to Martha E. WILLINS at Stewarts
            Neck
27 Jun 1883 J. Albert DOUGHERTY to Emma E. SMITH
26 Dec 1883 Thomas E. MORGAN to Annie C. SMITH
 6 Mar 1884 Charles W. HEATH to Letitia BLOODSWORTH at Monie
```

```
 1 Oct 1884 Theodore F. PUSEY to Mamie H. REESE
16 Dec 1884 Robert F. BRATTAN to Nellie H. DENNIS at
            residence of James U. DENNIS
25 Feb 1885 Andrew TYLER to Manie SHAW
10 Jun 1886 Archie McLANE to Mrs. Mary E. HEATH
13 Oct 1886 Rev. Oliver Hugh MURPHY to Sarah Esther DASHIELL
10 Nov 1886 John B. WALLER to Mrs. Virginia E. NEWMAN
24 Nov 1886 John Edgar BETTS to Cora Moore
 7 Feb 1888 John Edward GORSUCH to Mary Edith MILBOURN
18 Mar 1888 James D. BLOODSWORTH to Maggie McDANIEL
 4 Mar 1889 W. G. T. WALLER to Lucy L. STONE
 4 Sep 1889 John Henry LEWIS to Mary M. MUIR at Monie
 2 Nov 1889 Walter C. PENNOCK to Elizabeth Lewis
27 Nov 1889 John Barton YERBY to Nellie E. FURNISS at Monie
 1 Apr 1890 Edward F. BEAUCHAMP to Annie LANDING
18 Jun 190  James Preston KELLEY to Mary B. STONE
28 Oct 1890 Charles W. FITZGERALD to Margaret C. STEWART
28 Oct 1890 William HARVEY to Ellen Kerr STEWART
24 Dec 1890 Samuel J. DISHAROON to Annie E. WHEATLEY
22 Dec 1890 Denwood A. JONES to Nellie R. DENNIS
 3 Mar 1891 Irving S. ENNIS to Eliza V. REID
10 Jun 1891 Charles HERMON to Manda TURGG ?in Salisbury
20 Apr 1892 Henry M. MISTER to Nellie J. DASHIELL at Monie
 6 Dec 1892 Rufus MILLIGAN to Ellen A. BRITTINGHAM
13 Feb 1893 Rufus W. DASHIELL to Cecelia B. DENNIS
24 May 1893 Joshua WILSON to Leah HANDY
13 Dec 1893 Theodore B. REID to Olivia WHITLEY
```

DEATHS & BURIALS

```
 9 Jan 1708 William FISHER s/o JOHN FISHER
 3 Apr 1708 John FISHER s/o John
 6 Feb 1729 William SASSER
        1799 Nelly HOLBROOK w/o Samuel HOLBROOK age 20
15 Jul 1802 Sally STEWART d/o John STEWART & Jane STEWART

            BURIALS at ST ANDREWS CEMETERY unless
            otherwise indicated.

 7 Feb 1838 Mrs. DONE
11 Jun 1838 Susan Upshur JOHNSTON d/o Wm. W. & Rosina
16 Sep 1839 Henrietta Maria HYLAND d/o James C. & Mary
15 Dec 1840 Mrs. Sarah HYLAND
   Dec 1841 Mrs. E. A. R. WOOLFORD
   Dec 1841 Mrs. Priscilla HOLBROOK
   Dec 1841 Miss. Aususta HAYWARD
   Jun 1842 Mrs. A. McGRATH
   Jun 1842 Mrs. Rebecca DASHIELL
23 Jul 1842 George Upshur JOHNSTON s/o William
23 Jul 1842 Mrs. B. D. WALLER
   Aug 1842 Mrs. Ann WHITE
29 Sep 1842 Mrs. Sarah J. POLK
30 Sep 1842 Mrs. T. G. DASHIELL
11 Oct 1842 Mrs. Eleanor JONES
12 Sep 1843 James R. STEWART
13 Sep 1843 Ann MILES
17 Sep 1843 Eliza R. HYLAND
14 Aug 1843 Rev. Henry CROSDALE, d.12 August 1843
14 Nov 1842 Ann Thomas WALLER
25 Nov 1843 Mary Washington WALLER
13 Oct 1843 Mrs. DISHAROON age 79 yrs.
20 May 1844 Susan Esther DOUGHERTY d/o John DOUGHERTY & Mary
            DOUGHERTY age 5months
 3 Jul 1844 Susan Dixon BOWLAND d/o John BALLARD & Susan
            BALLARD age 14 years
16 Jul 1844 Charles DORSEY infant s/o Thomas DORSEY & Ellen
            DORSEY
 3 Aug 1844 Thomas G. DORSEY
 3 Oct 1844 John SMITH
 8 Dec 1844 William H. COLLIER
18 Feb 1845 John DONE
13 Mar 1845 Alexander Sidney CROCKETT son William CROCKETT
            age 6 years.
 6 Sep 1845 George Washington DASHIELL s/o George DASHIELL &
            Virginia DASHIELL age 3 years
25 Oct 1845 Sallie Elzey WATERS d/o E. WATERS & Ann Maria
            WATERS age 6 days
21 Apr 1846 Eliza WATERS wid/o Levin WATERS, died in
            Baltimore of consumption 17 April 1846, buried
            at Beachwood, family residence
 6 May 1846 Julia MILES d.5 May 1846 age 18 years
15 Oct 1846 Mrs. READ wid/o Robert READ
21 Feb 1847 Dr. James STEWART, d.19 Feb 1847 buried on his
```

```
                  farm in Manokin
11 Jun 1847 Mrs. Ellen WOOLFORD d. 9 Jun 1747
14 Aug 1847 Alexander CROCKETT s/o J. B. CROCKETT
 5 Sep 1847 Maria WATERS d/o Dr. W. E. WATERS
22 Oct 1847 Matilda Chase WOOLFORD
   Oct 1847 Annie WALLER d/o R. J. WALLER buried at farm of
                  George B. WALLER
 7 Jan 1849 Sarah Catherine d/o Rev. J.J. NICHOLSON age 8mo.
 7 Jan 1849 Stephen Coulbourn DASHIELL s/o G. W. DASHIELL
18 Jan 1849 Rosina Martin JOHNSTON d/o W. W. JOHNSTON &
                  Rosina d.16 Feb.1847
   Jul 1849 Frances SPENCER d/o M. W. SPENCER
24 Aug 1849 John JONES d.23 Aug 1849
18 Sep 1849 Mrs. Sallie B. DASHIELL
18 Oct 1849 Stewart JONES s/o Samuel S. JONES age 4
30 Oct 1849 Clark G. GARDNER d.28 Oct 1849
12 Mar 1850 Mary Eliza NICHOLSON w/o Rev. J.J. NICHOLSON
                  d.10 Mar 1850 age 31
 7 Jun 1850 Lawrence ROBERTS age 22 months
29 Sep 1850 William R. ATKINSON
11 Oct 1851 Caroline N. MILES
15 Feb 1852 Eliza KING
   Jun 1852 Elizabeth Dennis COTTMAN
21 Aug 1852 Frederick Stanley WATERS
21 Aug 1852 Mary DOUGHERTY buried Tyaskin Churchyard
21 Aug 1852 Biddy WALLER buried on Waller Farm in Monie
   Jul 1852 Dr. Henry HYLAND buried on his farm St. Peters
                  Creek
27 Sep 1852 Mrs. CARWIN d.26 Sep 1852 buried at home in
                  Hungary Neck.
28 Sep 1852 Harriet BALLARD d.27 Sep 1852
 1 Nov 1852 Robert BAILY d.31 Oct 1852
13 Nov 1852 Sarah G. CROSDALE d.12 Nov 1852
28 Apr 1853 Dr. C. E. JONES age 50  d.26 Apr 1853
27 May 1853 George S. ATKINSON age 32 d.24 May 1853
15 Jun 1853 Col. William JONES age 93 d.14 Jun 1853 buried
                  on Robert Dashiells farm in Monie Creek.
27 Jun 1853 John Henshaw MOORE s/o the rector of S. Parish
                  age 6 days d.25 Jun 1853
   Nov 1853 Arnold WATERS d/o Dr. W. E. WATERS age 14
   Jan 1854 Nancy LONG w/o Littleton LONG
27 Feb 1854 John H. KING age 51 d.25 Feb 1854
   Feb 1854 Samuel HOLBROOK buried on farm in Monie
   Feb 1854 G. Ballard R. WALLER buried on Waller farm
 1 Jan 1854 Levin MILLER d.31 Dec 1853 buried on his farm
                  near Princess Anne
20 Mar 1854 Mrs. James BRITTINGHAM d.19 May 1854 buried on
                  Brittingham farm
20 May 1854 Willie WATERS s/o W.E. WATERS d.19 May 1854
10 May 1854 Mrs. Eva HENRY buried at Berlin
29 Jun 1854 Dr. Robert K. W. DASHIELL d.28 Jun 1854 age 55
 2 Aug 1854 Elizabeth DENNIS child of James U. & C. DENNIS
 4 Aug 1854 Levin K. LEATHERBYURY d.in Baltimore buried at
                  Capt.McINTYRE'S in Hungary Neck
11 Aug 1854 Elizabeth E. CAUSEY  d.10 Aug 1854
```

3 Sep 1854 Mrs. Esther DOUGHERTY d.2 Sep 1854 age 54
buried at Tyaskin Churchyard
20 Oct 1854 Annie WOOLFORD d/o Levin & Ann WOOLFORD d.29 Oct
1854 buried at Col.Woolfords farm in Manokin
26 Dec 1854 Capt. Joseph BARCLAY d.25 Dec 1854 buried on his
farm at head of Wicomico Creek
6 Feb 1855 Elizabeth WHEATLY d/o Capt J. Wheatly
26 May 1855 Leah PINTO w/o John V. PINTO d.25 May1855 age 56
30 May 1855 Capt Theodore G. DASHIELL d.29 May 1855
16 Jul 1855 Mary Eliza HUGHES w/o Thomas of White Haven.
d.15 Jull 1855 age 26 buried St.Marys in Tyaskin
21 Aug 1855 Sarah G. HAYWARD d.20 Aug 1855 age 73
30 Oct 1855 Ezekiel Smith d.29 Oct 1855 buried at his home
10 Nov 1855 Washington WALLER d.9 Nov 1855 buried at Robert
Patterson's place in Monie
17 Nov 1855 Nelly STEWART d.15 Nov 1855 buried at St.Andrews
1 Jan 1856 Sarah HORNER d.31 Dec 1855 age 58 buried at
"California" in Hungary Neck
21 Jul 1856 Elizabeth R. POLLITT d.15 Jul1856 in Baltimore
age 50+. buried at Dr.Hylands St. Peters Creek
5 Dec 1856 Charlotte JONES d.6 Dec 1856 age 50
18 Jan 1857 Ann Maria ANDERSON w/o Stephen G. d.17 Jan 1857
21 Jan 1857 Hitch RENSCHER d.20 Jan 1857
9 Apr 1857 Aurelia DASHIELL w/o Hamden H.d.8 Apr1857 age 23
20 May 1857 Stephen G. ANDERSON d.19 May 1857
28 May 1857 Aurelia MILES w/o Alfred M. d.27 May 1857
31 Aug 1857 Levin WHITE d.21 Aug 1857 buried on Robert
Pattersons farm
28 Sep 1857 Emily DIX d/o Thomas d.27 Sep 1857 age 6months
6 Oct 1857 Leah Bess JONES d/o Mrs.Media d.5 Oct 1857
15 Oct 1857 Dr. Littleton D. HANDY d.14 Oct 1857 age 48
15 Oct 1857 Alpheus CROCKETT s/o William CROCKETT & Ann d.17
Oct 1857 age 4 months
28 Jul 1858 Jane STEWART d/o Dr. James d.27 Jul 1858 age 36
24 Nov 1858 Stephen DRURA d.23 Nov 1858 age over 50
25 Nov 1858 Robert DENNIS d.24 Nov 1858
3 Dec 1858 George Tubman HARRIS d.2 Dec 1858 age 19
1 Apr 1859 George Henry JONES d.30 Mar 1859 age 32 buried
on Dr. Thomas W. Stone's place in Wicomico
1 Oct 1859 Margaret W. JOHNSTON d.25 Sep 1859 age 84
24 Mar 1860 George BALLARD d.23 Mar 1860 age 60
10 May 1860 No name BOWLAND d.1 May 1860 age 67
22 Jun 1860 William J. BYRD d.Aiken S.C.18 Jun 1860 age 31
22 Aug 1860 Sallie F. COVINGTON d.21 Aug 1860 age 22
25 Aug 1860 Maggie L. T. MILLS d.24 Aug 1860 age 19 months
31 Aug 1860 Eugneia WILSON d.30 Aug 1860 age 16 months
14 Nov 1860 Ida LARMOUR d.13 Aug 1860 age 4 months
27 Dec 1860 Rufus DOUGHERTY drowned 25 Dec 1860 age 13
buried at his home on St. Peters Creek.
10 Mar 1861 Mary Louisa WOOLFORD d.8 Mar 1861 age 21 months
buried at the Methodist burying ground
1 Apr 1861 Virginia Stewart CROCKETT d.31 Mar 1861 age 6mo.
15 Apr 1861 Margaret NICHOLS d.12 Apr1861 in Baltimore 73yrs
6 May 1861 Cecilia DENNIS w/o James U.d.5 May 1861 age 35
25 Jun 1861 John Franklin PRICE d.21 Jun 1861 age 20 buried

```
                   on George B. Waller's in Monie
10 Jul 1861 John William WALKER d.9 Jul 1861 age 6 months
20 Jul 1861 Dr. Thomas D. JONES d.19 Jul 1861 age 72 buried
            at Robert Dashiell's in Monie
13 Aug 1861 Sarah JOHNSTON d. 12 Aug 1861 age 18
14 Aug 1861 Julius RIAL d.12 Aug 1861 age about 23 buried at
            St. Mary's Church, Tyaskin
27 Sep 1861 Dr.Matthias SUDLER d.25 Sep 1861 age 31
27 Nov 1861 Joseph DASHIELL d.26 Nov 1861 age 1 year
17 Dec 1861 Henrietta ATKINSON d.15 Dec 1861 at Almodington
            age 67
14 Jan 1862 Matthias J. SUDLER d.13 Jan 1862 age 2
19 Jan 1862 Thomas H. MORRIS d.17 Jan 1862 age 18
27 Jan 1862 Amanda JONES d.25 Jan 1862 age 56 buried at
            Robert Dashiell's in Monie
 9 Feb 1862 George D. ATKINSON d.6 Feb 1862 age 2
 5 Mar 1862 Eliza LANKFORD d. 1 Mar 1862 age 15
19 Mar 1862 John WOOLFORD d.17 Mar 1862 age about 58 buried
            in Manokin
29 Mar 1862 Mrs. Media JONES d.28 Mar 1862 age 73
 8 Jul 1862 Mrs. Rufus M. PARSONS d. 7 Mar 1862
31 Jul 1862 Harriett Ethlan DASHIELL d/o Cadmus & Henrietta
            d.30 Jul 1862 buried in family Cemetary on
            Wetipkin Creek
 5 Aug 1862 Frederick GREEN d.4 Aug 1862 age about 65 buried
            Whitney farm near Grace Church
29 Jan 1863 Col. Joseph Stewart COTTMAN d.28 Jan 1863 age 60
14 Feb 1863 Joseph Covell LONG d.5 Feb 1863 New York age 34
28 Feb 1863 Henry E. L. MORRIS d.27 Feb 1863 age 38
31 May 1863 Mrs. RENSHAW w/o Thaddeus W. d.30 May 1863
            buried at home of William A. D. Bounds
23 Jun 1863 Mrs. Mary E. MILBOURN d.21 Jun 1863 age 28
 8 Jul 1863 Maria WALLER w/o Robert J. d.7 Jul 1863 age 46
            buried at George Waller's on Monie
21 Jul 1863 Infant child of J. H. RISLEY of d.20 Jul 1863
            age 4 months buried at Westover, Back Creek
31 Jul 1863 Edward Pomeroy SUDLER s/o Joseph & Candace d.30
            Jul 1863 age nearly 4 months
14 Aug 1863 Mrs. Leah BEAUCHAMP d.12 Aug 1863 age 68 buried
            at John Woolford's on Monie
18 Aug 1863 Clara JONES d/o James W. d.17 Aug 1863 age 2mo.
 1 Oct 1863 Mrs. Purnell TOADVINE d.28 Sep 1863 age 48
            buried near Salisbury
10 Oct 1863 Leroy ANDERSON d.27 Sep 1863 age 21
23 Oct 1863 George NENTWICK d.21 Oct 1863 age 50
31 Dec 1863 Thomas James LYNCH s/o Joseph E. LYNCH of White
            Haven d.28 Dec 1863 age 2 buried at Rockawalkin
 9 Jan 1864 Eliza Russum ATKINSON d/o Isaac S. d.4 Jan 1864
            age 21 months
22 Jan 1864 Alice SMITH d/o William T. SMITH d.22 Jan 1864
            of scarlet fever age 6 buried on farm at St.
            Peters Creek
24 Jan 1864 Martin SMITH d.24 Jan 1864 age 4, same as above
25 Jan 1864 Mary SMITH d.25 Jan 1864, age 8, same as above
27 Jan 1864 Samuel SMITH d.27 Jan 1864 age 12, same as above
```

```
28 Jan 1864 Henry SMITH d.27 Jan 1864 age 10,same as above
 6 Feb 1864 John R. STURGIS killed in steam mill 4 Feb.1864
            about 41 buried in churchyard at New Town
20 Feb 1864 Henrietta BRITTINGHAM w/o William J.BRITTINGHAM
            d.17 Feb 1864 age 38
21 Feb 1864 Ellen HASTINGS d/o W. H. d.18 Feb 1854 age 8
24 Feb 1864 Nathan James LANKFORD d.22 Feb 1864 age 20
12 Mar 1864 Rev. James Murray STONE d/o Dr. James d.11 March
            1864 age 4
 7 Apr 1864 Annie BELL d/o John H. d.6 Apr 1864 age 7
 2 May 1864 Margaret Wilson DENNIS d/o Dr. George R. d.30
            Apr 1864 age 3
30 May 1864 William Polk BELL s/o John H. BELL d.29 May 1864
            age about 8 months
26 Jun 1864 John Hambleton LONG s/o L. d. 25 Jun 1864 age 5
10 Jul 1864 Infant d/o Joseph SMITH d.9 Jul 1864 age 4 mo.
            buried in Methodist burying ground
27 Jul 1864 Ann WHITE w/o Henry A. d.25 Jul 1864 age 40
            buried in Presbyterian burying ground
31 Jul 1864 Laura Griswold SUDLER d/o Joseph d.30 Jul 1874
            age 3 weeks
 2 Oct 1864 Mrs. Rosa WALTER d.30 Sep 1864 age 79 buried in
            Tyaskin distict.
23 Feb 1865 Edward D. BALLARD d.20 Feb 1864 age 43 buried at
            St. Peters Creek
25 Mar 1865 Charles W. WHITTINGTON d. 20 Mar 1865 in
            Baltimore age 20
 4 Apr 1865 John SMITH d. 12 Apr 1865 age 94
 3 May 1865 James W. COSTEN d. 1 May 1865
27 May 1865 Elijah B. ADAMS d. 26 May 1865 age about 48
27 Jun 1865 Mrs. MADDUX w/o Edward d. 26 Jun 1865 buried at
            Maddux farm east of town
20 Aug 1865 Miss Priscilla DASHIELL d.15 Aug 1865 age 38
 2 Sep 1865 Hobart JOHNSTON s/o William W. d.1 Sep1865 age12
 4 Sep 1865 James Alfred COX grandchild of James ANDERSON d.
            2 Sep 1865 age 6 months
11 Sep 1865 George Matthias DASHIELL eldest s/o Cadmus d.8
            Sep 1865 age 20 buried at Wetipquin Creek
18 Sep 1865 Thomas J. WHITE d.in Baltimore age 61 buried on
            Robert Pattersons farm in Monie
21 Oct 1865 Clara Wilson TULL d/o J. F. & Esther d. 20 Oct
            1865 age 3 months
26 Oct 1865 Mary Amanda SMITH d/o Joseph F. d.25 Oct 1854
            age 4 buried in Methodist burying ground
 8 Nov 1865 Alphonsa SUDLER w/o Matthias d. 6 Nov 1865
22 Dec 1865 William Wilson JOHNSTON d.20 Dec 1865 age 58, a
            vestryman for 34 years and built the St. Andrews
            Church tower and presented the organ
19 Jan 1865 William Catherwood WALLER s/o Washington d. 17
            Jan 1866 age 11 buried at George B. Wallers
27 Jan 1866 James Upshur DENNIS s/o George W. DENNIS d.25
            Jan 1866 age 21 months
29 Jan 1866 William MILES d.27 Jan 1866 nearly 85 buried in
            family cemetary near his home. Vestryman
12 Feb 1866 Mrs. Sophia E. HANDY d.22 Feb 1866 age 54
```

17 Feb 1866 Miss Eliza RUSSUM d. 15 Feb 1866 age 77
23 Feb 1866 Mrs. Annie W. JONES d.21 Feb 1866 age 77
13 Mar 1866 Mrs. Henrietta GARDNER d.11 Mar 1866 age 68
20 Mar 1866 Littleton S. WHITE d.19 Mar 1866 age 68
27 Apr 1866 WilliamAnna WOOLFORD w/o William d.25 Apr 1868
17 Jul 1866 Miss Jane COTTMAN d.15 Jul 1866 over 85 buried
         in family place at Wicomico Creek
19 Jul 1866 John COVINGTON d.28 July 1855 over 70 buried at
         family place on "The Ridge"
23 Jul 1866 Clarisa DASHIELL w/o Nathaniel d.22 Jul 1866·
         buried in churchyard in Quantico
 5 Aug 1866 Alfred Jones STEWART s/o Dr. William d. 4 Aug
         1855 age 6 months
29 Aug 1866 Esther Wilson Tull w/o Joshua F.A. d.27 Aug 1866
 1 Sep 1866 William W. BOWLAND d. 21 Aug 1866 age about 51
 1 Sep 1866 William Murray Stone WHITE s/o Henry A. d.31 Aug
         1866 age 21 buried Presbyterian Burying ground
 5 Sep 1866 Mrs. Eleanor T. WAILES d. 3 Sep 1866 age 74
 8 Sep 1866 Eva CHATHAM d/o Frank & Elizabeth d. 7 Sep 1866
         age 10
 9 Sep 1866 Miss Harriet CROCKETT
 1 Oct 1866 Henry Wyatt WHITE s/o Henry A. d. 29 Sep 1855
         age 19 buried Presbyterian burying ground
20 Oct 1866 James C. HYLAND d. 17 Oct 1866 age 26
24 Oct 1866 Henrietta Gardner BRITTINGHAM w/o W. J. d.22 Oct
         1866 age 30
31 Oct 1866 Miss Ellen HANDY d.30 Oct 1866 age 27
 4 Nov 1866 Mrs. Esther LAWRENCE d. 3 Nov 1866 age 76
 7 Nov 1866 Alfred H. JONES d.5 Nov 1866 age 58
 8 Nov 1866 John Henry STEWART d. 6 Nov 1866 age 54
25 Nov 1866 Eugene SMITH d. 23 Nov 1866 age 29
30 Dec 1866 John DOUGHERTY d.29 Dec 1866 age 52
12 Jan 1867 William L. HOLBROOK d. 20 Jan 1867 age 44
10 Feb 1867 Lammie YERBY d. 8 Feb 1857 age 10
17 Mar 1867 Sydney S. JONES d. 14 Mar 1867 age 34
13 May 1867 Edwin Polk DASHIELL d. 10 May 1867 age 3
16 Jul 1867 Miss Eleanor A. DASHIELL d. 14 Jul 1867
30 Aug 1867 Henrietta LONG d/o L. d.29 Aug 1867 age 8 months
 1 Sep 1867 Norman Dashiell WANGEMAN d. 31 Aug 1867 age 3
 6 Sep 1867 Jacob Emory NEWMAN d.5 Sep 1867 age 37 buried at
         cemetery at Baltimore
18 Oct 1867 Bessie Gardner BRITTINGHAM d/o William J. d. 16
         Oct 1857 age 1
20 Oct 1867 Theodore Dashiell HOLBROOK s/o Thomas W. d. 15
         Oct 1867 age 8 months
23 Jan 1868 Dr. Francis GALE d.2 Jan 1868 age 35
16 Apr 1868 Jane W. DASHIELL w/o James T.d.14 Apr1868 age 31
27 Jul 1868 Henry A. WHITE d.25 Jul 1868 about age 50 buried
         Presbyterian burying ground
21 Aug 1868 William G. WOOLFORD d.19 Aug 1868 age about 61
 1 Nov 1868 Mary HARRIS d/o Littleton d. 30 Oct 1868 buried
         near house in Hungary Neck
31 Feb 1869 Emily DENNIS d/o George R. d.19 Feb 1869 age 6
 5 Apr 1869 Robert W. DOUGHERTY d.2 Apr 1869 age about 50
 7 Apr 1869 Thomas Oliver NEWMAN s/o Sidney b. 6 Apr 1869

age 1 week
21 Jul 1869 Mason ABBOTT d. 20 Jul 1869 age 87
21 Jul 1869 Robert Ritchie CHATTAM s/o Thomas F. d.20 Jul
1869 age 9 months
31 Jul 1869 Nathalie LONG d/o Littleton d.Washington age14mo
9 Aug 1869 Samuel W. JONES d.7 Aug 1869 age 65
10 Aug 1869 Charles ABBOTT d.8 Aug 1869
Sep 1869 Mrs. Elizabeth A. CHATTAM
26 Nov 1869 Helen S. PATTERSON w/o R. d.24 Nov 1869 age 71
buried at farm in Monie
Feb 1870 Alfred M. MILES
20 Oct 1870 George D. WALLER d.19 Oct 1870 age 81 buried at
farm in Little Monie
28 Oct 1870 Elizabeth W. DASHIELL w/o H.H. d.26 Oct 1870
age 30
9 Nov 1870 Sidney WHEATLY s/o Joseph d.8Nov 1870 age 6mo.
17 Nov 1870 Robert JONES of George d.15 Nov 1870 age 74
8 Dec 1870 Seth B. DASHIELL d.7 Dec 1870 age 50
8 Apr 1871 Robert H. JONES s/o Robert of George d. 6 Apr
1871 age 34
2 May 1871 Littleton HARRIS d.1 May 1871 age 71 buried on
his farm in Hungary Neck
2 Jun 1871 Henry BRISCOE s/o Henry & Esther d. 1 Jun 1871
age 4
21 Aug 1871 William Jones WALLER s/o W. T. & Mary Ellen age
18 months buried Robert Dashiells farm on Monie
26 Aug 1871 John Samuel HOLBROOK d.25 Aug 1871 age 46
6 Oct 1871 Mrs. Harriett E. HYLAND d. 4 Oct 1871 age about
70 buried on farm on St. Peter's Creek
10 Dec 1871 Mrs. Caroline A. GALE d.8 Dec 1871 age 70 or 73
29 Dec 1871 Randall JAGGARD d.26 Dec 1871 age 46
5 Feb 1872 Sydnham HYLAND d.in Baltimore age 27
7 Feb 1872 Eleanor WALLER w/o George B. deceased d.5 Feb
1872 age 75 buried on farm in Little Monie
19 Feb 1872 Julia SMITH d/o William H. d.17 Feb 1872 age 9
buried in Methodist graveyard Princess Anne
25 Mar 1872 Susan W. BAILY w/o Wm. A. d.23 Mar 1872 age 47
23 Apr 1872 James Washington COSTEN s/o James W. deceased
b.21 Apr 1872 age 8
5 May 1872 Mrs. Mary W. WHITTINGTON d. 3 May 1872
29 May 1872 Mrs. Drusilla GREEN d.28 May 1872 age 75 buried
on Whitney farm near Grace Church
20 Aug 1872 Robert Waters LLOYD s/o George W. of Whitehaven
age 7 months
21 Aug 1872 Emily May SMITH d/o Wm.H. d.20 Aug 1872 age 15
months buried Methodist graveyard
31 Aug 1872 Miss Priscilla WHITNEY d.30 Aug 1872 age 81
buried on Whitney farm near Grace Church
28 Sep 1872 Joseph SUDLER d. 26 Sep 1872 age 44
7 Dec 1872 Lemuel BROOKS s/o Caleb & Margaret A. d. 5 Dec
1872 age 5
4 Apr 1873 Dr. Henry BRISCOE d.3 Apr 1873 age 42
1 May 1873 Annie Virginia SLEMMONS w/o J. Edwin d/o Emeline
J. Morris d.30 Apr 1873 age 23
7 May 1873 Robert Sydney Miles s/o Matthias drowned 6 May

1873 age 13 buried at farm 3 miles east of town
6 Sep 1873 Louise Oates MUIR w/o Robert H. d. 4 Sep 1873
24 Sep 1873 William S. TYLER d.23 Sep 1873 buried Rock Creek
Methodist churchyard
6 Dec 1873 James Anderson HICKMAN d.4 Dec 1873 in
Philadelphia age 3
10 Dec 1873 Eliza COVINGTON wid/o Isaac d.5 Dec 1873 in
Salisbury age 58
13 Jan 1874 Miss Margaret TEAGLE d.11 Jan 1874 age 70 buried
in Presbyterian burying ground
14 Apr 1874 Mary Elizabeth SMITH s/o Joseph F. d.12 Apr 1874
age about 54
5 Jun 1874 William PUSEY s/o Edwin & Kate d.4 Jun 1874 2mo.
22 Jul 1874 Alice Gale STEWART d/o Dr. William d.5 Aug 1874
age nearly 3
28 Aug 1874 Samuel Ker STEWART s/o Wm. d.25 Aug 1874 age 1
31 Oct 1874 George H. RENSHAW s/o Thaddeus d.29 Oct 1874 age
6 buried near house Wm.A.D.Bounds Hungary Neck
5 Dec 1874 Emeline J. MORRIS wid/o Henry E.L. d.4 Dec 1874
age about 54
24 Dec 1874 No name d/o Littleton LONG d.23 Dec 1874 in
Philadelphia
5 Jan 1875 James ANDERSON d 31 Dec 1875 in Philadelphia
29 Jul 1875 Miss Ellen Polk WOOLFORD d.27 Jul 1875 age 28
buried on farm on Manokin
3 Aug 1875 Sarah Murray STONE d/o Thomas W. d.1 Aug 1874
age 23
17 Aug 1875 Ernest COVINGTON s/o Scott & Ellen d.15 Aug 1873
age 1 week
1 Sep 1875 Henrietta E. JONES w/o Robert of George d.31 Aug
1875 age about 63
3 Nov 1875 Thomas W. KELLY d.1 Nov 1875 buried in Dames
Quarter
4 Nov 1875 John MILLER d.2 Nov 1875 age about 73
20 Oct 1875 Henry Silliman WALLER s/o William d.18 Oct 1875
age 3 mo. buried on Robert Dashiell's farm
1 Jan 1876 George Albert HEATH s/o Thomas d.30 Dec 1875 age
nearly 3, buried at Habenhab near Monie Creek
12 Feb 1876 Jeanette WHITE w/o Silas d.9 Feb 1876 age nearly
52 buried on farm of Robert Patterson
17 Feb 1876 Dr. Edward Reid WALLER s/o Robert J. d.15 Feb
1876 on Deals Island age 31 buried at old
homestead on Little Monie
1 Jun 1876 Miss Henrietta Ann Holland Reid WALLER d. 30 May
1876 age 59
18 Jun 1876 Harriett ROBERTSON d/o H. H. & Maggie d.16 Jun
1876 age 21 months 8 days
20 Aug 1876 William Edgar BRITTINGHAM s/o William J. d.19
Aug 1876 age 18 years 11 months
22 Sep 1876 Mrs. Elizabeth H. BROWN dressmaker d.20 Sep 1876
age about 54 buried Methodist burial ground
4 Nov 1876 Harry SUDLER s/o Dr. Matthias & Alphonsa
19 Jan 1877 Carrie HOLBROOK d/o Thomas W. d.14 Jan 1873 in
Minnesota age 16
19 Jan 1877 Mrs. Rosina M. JOHNSTON d.17 Jan 1877 age 67

```
14 Feb 1877 Albert A. WALLER d.18 feb 1877 age 50 buried at
            homestead in Little Monie
20 Feb 1877 Sallie YERBY w/o Lemuel d. 19 Feb 1877
 6 Apr 1877 Constance Chaille LONG d/o Littleton d. 4 Apr
            1877 age 6 1/2 months
21 May 1877 James T. McDORMAN d.20 May1877 buried in Dames
            Quarter
 9 Jun 1877 William Charles BARTON s/o Rector John O. d. 7
            June 1877 age 17
 6 Aug 1877 Mrs. Charlotte KING d. 5 Aug 1877 age 72
 6 Oct 1877 George W. DIXON d.6 Oct 1877
13 Jan 1878 John Done KING d.12 Jan 1879 age 42
 1 Mar 1878 Miss Sallie GILLIS d.27 Feb 1878 age 63
 5 Mar 1878 Mrs. Susan OATES d. 3 Mar 1878
27 Mar 1878 Washington MUIR d.25 Mar 1878 age 22
 1 Apr 1878 Silas WHITE d.7 Apr 1878 age 70 buried on farm
            on Monie
12 Apr 1878 Virginia Catherine MUIR w/o John age 24
16 Jul 1878 Sidney G. BOWLAND d.15 Jul 1878 age 45
 4 Aug 1878 Anne Rebecca PRICE w/o William A. d.2 Aug 1878
            age 44, buried White family graveyard
28 Sep 1878 Mary E. RENSHAW w/o Thaddeus d. 27 Sep 1878 age
            about 40 buried at home of Wm. A. D. Bounds
            Hungary Neck
13 Sep 1878 Eugenie Annie GROSCUP d.12 Sep 1878 age 10 days
 9 Feb 1879 Franklin E. WALLER d.8 Feb 1878 age 49 buried at
            old homestead Little Monie
25 Feb 1879 Esther Jane WILSON w/o James W. d.23 Feb 1878
            age 58
21 Mar 1879 William A. D. BOUNDS d.20 Mar 1879 age 57 buried
            at homestead in Hungary neck
27 Apr 1879 W. Scott COVINGTON d. 2 Apr 1879 age 31
29 Jun 1879 Julius C. ABBOTT d.28 Jun 1879 age 30
 6 Sep 1879 George R. BALLARD d.4 Sep 1879 age nearly 85
            buried at home in St. Peters Creek
 8 Sep 1879 Benjamin PARSONS d.7 Sep 1879 age 83 buried
            Parsons Cemetery in Salisbury
13 Sep 1879 Clement RIALL d.11 Sep 1879 age 25 buried St.
            Marys churchyard in Tyaskin
19 Oct 1879 William Wilson WISE d.15 Oct 1879
 3 Nov 1879 Kendall B. PARSONS d.2 Nov 1879 age 68
 7 Nov 1879 Temperance BOUNDS wid/o Wm. A. D. d.5 Nov 1879
            age 76 buried family ground Wicomico River
26 Oct 1879 John C. HORSEY d.24 Oct 1876 age about 66,buried
            family ground Annamessex
19 Feb 1880 Edward MATTHEWS buried "Peach Blossom" farm
30 Mar 1880 Upshur JOHNSTON of Baltimore s/o Wm.W. d.28 Mar
            1880 age 35
28 Jun 1880 Louisa Harris BOUNDS w/o James H. d.27 Jun 1880
            age 77 buried Grace Churchyard
30 Sep 1880 Miss Harriett WHITNEY d.29 Sep 1880 age nearly
            90, buried Grace Churchyard
 1 Oct 1880 Annie PARSONS d/o Rufus d.29 Sep 1880 in
            Baltimore
15 Dec 1880 Littleton LONG Sr. d.13 Dec 1880 age 84
```

20 Jan 1881 John C. HANDY s/o Littleton d.28 Jan 1881 age 42
13 Feb 1881 Mortimer LONG d.11 Feb 1881 in New york age 43
12 Mar 1881 Henry Eugene CURTIS s/o Levin H. d.10 Mar 1881
            age 4
13 Mar 1881 Mrs. Anna Maria POTTER d.10 Mar 1881 age about
            45 buried All Saints Churchyard Monie
21 Mar 1881 Whittington POLLITT d. 19 Mar 1881 age 60 buried
            John Woolford's burial ground
20 Apr 1881 Col. John GALE d.18 Apr 1882 age 55
21 Apr 1881 Mary FISHER d.19 Apr 1881 buried Methodist Cem.
 1 Jun 1881 Samuel BOUNDS s/o James d.31 May 1881 age 17
            buried Grace Churchyard
16 Jun 1881 Mary Culbreath POLK w/o E. G. d.14 Jun 1881 age
            about 30 buried Presbyterian burial ground   4
Jun 1881 George Bernard GROSCUP d.2 Jun 1881 age 9mo
            buried Mount Vernon District
28 Aug 1881 John Barton HUMPHREYS s/o W. d.22 Aug 1881 9mos.
29 Sep 1881 Nathan James LANGFORD d.25 Sep 1881 age 74
 1 Sep 1881 Dr. William STEWART d.29 Nov 1881 age 55
31 Dec 1881 Maria MILLER mother of Rev. John S. d.26 Dec
            1881 about 75 years old
 3 Mar 1882 Kate Rosalie PUSEY d/o Edwin & Catherine d. 2
            Mar 1882 age 5
30 Jul 1882 Susan Esther DOUGHERTY d. 27 Jul 1882 in
            Baltimore age 27
 9 Aug 1882 Mary K. LONG w/o Littleton Jr.d 7 Aug 1882
14 Aug 1882 Hon. George R. DENNIS late U.S. Senator d. 12
            Aug 1882
 4 Sep 1882 Jesse PUSEY s/o Edwin & Catherine E. d. 3 Sep
            1882 age 7
31 Oct 1882 Mrs. COVINGTON wid/o the late John d. 29 oct
            1872 age 78
12 Nov 1882 Levin R. BOWLAND d.11 Nov 1882 age 62
22 Nov 1882 Capt. George DAVY d.20 Nov 1882 age 84 buried at
            home near Fairmount,a worthy old gentleman
19 Jan 1883 Mary Ellen WALLER w/o William Thomas d.17 Jan
            1883 buried Robert Dashiell's on Monie
30 Jan 1883 Thomas W. HEATH d.25 Jan 1883 buried All Saints
            churchyard in Monie
 2 Feb 1883 William LLOYD d.21 Jan 1883 age nearly 83 buried
            Grace Church at Mt Vernon
14 Mar 1883 Mrs. Jane D. McELHINY d. 12 Mar 1883 age 73
26 Mar 1883 Mary E. SMITH w/o Jack d.24 Mar 1883 age 84
17 May 1883 James B. ABBOTT d.15 May 1883 age 35
 3 Sep 1883 Henry LOKEY d.2 Sep 1883 age 60 buried All
            Saints churchyard at Monie
10 Oct 1883 Horace Norman JONES d. 8 Oct 1883 age 23
30 Oct 1883 Dr. Christopher Harrison Hyland d.28 oct 883 age
            over 60 buried on farm on St.Peter's Creek
18 Dec 1883 George OATES an Irishman d. 15 Dec 1883 age
            about 60
22 Apr 1884 William J. DENNIS s/o Dr. G. A. d.18 Apr 1884
            age 27
20 Sep 1884 Elsie LAWSON d/o P.H. & Amelia M. d. 19 Sep 1884
            age 9 months

69

```
 4 Dec 1884 Miss Elizabeth S. DASHIELL d.2 Dec 1884 age 72
23 Apr 1885 Sallie DOUGHERTY w/o Robert W. d.17 Apr 1885 in
            Baltimore age 49
 2 Apr 1885 May E. CROSDALE w/o Rev. Henry d.23 Apr 1885 in
            Snow Hill
15 May 1885 Miss Adeline MILES d.13 May 1885
   Dec 1884 Miss Elizabeth Sarah DASHIELL age 71
18 Dec 1884 Harriett T. W. DASHIELL w/o Cadmus age 65
 2 Jul 1885 Mrs. Capt. WHEATLY age 76 buried on Manokin
 3 Aug 1885 Susan H. ATKINSON w/o Isaac S. age 64
 7 Oct 1885 Sally A. KING w/o Dr. John Trippe age 56 buried
            on St. Peters Creek
 7 Oct 1885 Lemuel YERBY age 55
   Dec 1885 Infant child of Samuel & Nannie C. LANKFORD
29 Jun 1886 Alexander Furniss buried All Saints in Monie
       1885 William H. BROWN
       1885 Wife of John Bell WALLER Esq.
   Sep 1886 Isaac W. LOCKEY age 8 wks. buried Monie church
 5 Oct 1886 Oscar MORGAN age 10 months
 6 Oct 1886 Mary LOCKEY age 2 yrs. buried Monie churchyard
11 Oct 1885 Mrs. Amelia A. BREWINGTON age 76 buried Monie
 2 Nov 1886 Avelon LAWSON age 5 weeks
 1 Jan 1887 Mrs. Elizabeth MOORE age 24 buried Parsons
            Cemetary in Salisbury
 1 Jan 1887 Mrs. Martha PENNOCK age 30 buried Monie
 5 Jan 1887 Mary R. PATTERSON age 63 buried private ground
20 Jan 1887 Mrs. Sallie B. DASHIELL age 27 buried
            Presbyterian churchyard Pr. Anne
 1 Mar 1887 John BREWINGTON age 90 buried Monie
 7 May 1887 Mrs. Agusta LANKFORD age 90 buried private
            grave yard near Pocomoke
12 Jul 1887 Mrs. Col. James POLK age 87
20 Aug 1887 Mrs. Mary E. DORMAN age 57
31 Aug 1887 Nellie G. HOLBROOK age about 52
18 Dec 1887 William A. BAILEY age 69
20 Jan 1888 Mrs. Mary RENSHAW age 90
 5 May 1888 Thomas G. WOOLFORD age 78 buried private grave
14 May 1888 Mrs. Annie McGRATH age 32 buried at Grace Church
 9 Jun 1888 Oscar RIALL age 19 buried St. Marys Church at
            Tyaskin
13 Aug 1888 Mrs. Caroline WOOLFORD age 81 buried at family
            ground in Manokin
30 Aug 1888 Ira S. HEATH age 17 months
14 Oct 1888 Walter G. JONES age 47 buried private ground at
            St. Peters Creek
13 Oct 1888 Washington Ballard age over 60
12 Jun 1889 Daisy YERBY age 8
11 Aug 1889 Mary Estelle COVINGTON age 5 weeks
10 Jan 1890 Mannie WHITTINGTON age 18 buried St. Marys
            Church in Pocomoke City
 6 Mar 1890 Martha A. JONES age 64
 8 Apr 1890 John B. WALLER buried All Saints Ch. in Monie
11 May 1890 Mrs. Henrietta J. LAWSON
25 Jun 1890 Mrs. Samuel PUSEY age 45 buried All Saints Monie
28 Jun 1890 Mrs. Julia A. COLLINS age 74
```

```
30 Sep 1890 Col. Levin WOOLFORD age 71
16 Oct 1890 Archer PUSEY age 8 buried All Saints
16 Oct 1890 Infant of Sidney REVELL age 2 weeks
30 Oct 1890 William T. GREEN age 28 buried Grace Church
            Wicomico Parish
12 Feb 1891 Henry Matthew HEATH age 3 weeks buried All
            Saints
 5 Mar 1891 Mrs. Mary Ann DASHIELL age 70
14 Mar 1891 Willie Carr PUSEY age 14 mo. buried Grace Church
20 Mar 1891 Chandlette Ailine MINER infant d/o M. W.
13 Apr 1891 Mrs. Charles YOUNG age 24 buried Grace Church
26 Apr 1891 Mrs. Dr. James STONE age 60
29 Apr 1891 Reinterred remains of Rev. Dr. BARTON from
            Easton
15 Jun 1891 Robert J. WALLER age 72 buried in Monie
22 Jul 1891 Hattie Virginia YOUNG age 3 1/2 months buried
            Grace Church
23 Jul 1891 Mrs. Sallie R. JONES age 82
23 Aug 1891 Eleanor Louise LAWSON age 3months buried All
            Saints in Monie
 2 Dec 1891 F. Herbert WATERS buried All Saints
14 Dec 1891 Robert Bruce WALLER age 6 months buried in Monie
23 Dec 1891 John BELL age 69
 8 Jan 1892 Mrs. Mary E. Coulborne age 86
22 Mar 1891 Ann Emily Miner age 40 buried All Saints
27 Jun 1892 George H. PALMATORY age 65
29 Jun 1892 John WILLIS age 72 buried at old Waller place on
            Monie
 6 Aug 1892 Mary Edith WALKER age 3 months
 7 Aug 1892 Lucy Gillis KELLEY age 15 mos. buried All Saints
18 Nov 1892 Rev. Robert J. CLUTE age 60 rector of Stepney
            Spring Hill Parish buried St. Stephens in
            Quantico
22 Dec 1892 James W. WILSON age 75
10 Jan 1893 Sallie A. DOUGHERTY age 37
27 Mar 1893 Mrs. Mati Sarah NELSON age 33 buried All Saints
28 Apr 1893 John W. HUMPHREYS age 60
14 Sep 1893 Hilda BEAUCHAMP age 19mos.buried St Stephens
24 Nov 1893 John B. WALLER age 50 buried with familly Monie
30 Nov 1893 Mrs. Annie LANKFORD
15 Dec 1893 Thomas E. MORGAN age 9 months
 5 Jan 1894 Mrs. Marie S. HOLBROOK age 78
20 Jul 1850 Capt. John A. BOWLAND d.18 July 1850
30 Dec 1850 Dr. KER
   Aug 1850 Mrs. Isabella WALLER w/o Ballard
15 Oct 1850 Alexander JONES Sr.
20 Oct 1850 Henry James HYLAND d.18 Oct 1850
```

COMMUNICANTS

Only those members who were removed for any reason

1846

Tubman SUDLER removed to Coventry parish
Miss Mary E. WALTON removed to Grace Church Hungary Neck
Dr. Littleton D. HANDY and wife removed to Coventry Parish
Mrs. Littleton L. WHITE removed to Baltimore
Mrs. William MILES, deceased
Mrs. Elizabeth TOLBERT, removed
Mrs. Nancy MILES, deceased
Mrs. COTTMAN of Wicomico Creek, deceased
Jonadab LAURENCE, deceased
Joseph WHITNEY, deceased
Mrs. Thomas K. CARROLL, removed
George JOHNSTON, deceased
Mrs. CROCKETT, stricken off
Mrs. BEAUCHAMP removed to Coventry parish
Miss Charlotte Henry removed to Coventry parish
Miss Henrietta Long removed to COVENTRY
Levin C. WHITE stricken off

1843

Samuel K. DASHIELL, removed
Mrs. READ died 14 Oct 1846
Dr. James STEWART, deceased
Joshua REESE and wife removed to Baltimore
George JOHNSTON, deceased
Miss Mary Ann RIAL, removed
Mrs. SEABREEZE, removed
Miss Mathilda STEWART removed and married
Miss Mary Ann STANLEY, removed
Mrs. Martha SPENCER, removed
William MILES, removed

1847

Col. William JONES deceased 10 Jun 1853
Lemuel G. HOLBROOK, deceased
Mrs. Dr. HYLAND, removed
Mrs. Sarah B. DASHIELL, removed
Miss Elizabeth JONES, removed
S. K. STEWART removed to Coventry Parish
William REDDICK, deceased
Mrs. DORSEY, removed
Levin TRADER and wife of Wicomico, removed
Mrs. NICHOLS, removed
Mrs. Betsy DISHAROON
Mrs. Betsy ALLEN of Dames Quarter, deceased
Mrs. Scott DASHIELL, deceased
Patrick CAUSEY, removed
Mrs. PURNELL, removed
Lucy R. DRISKELL, removed
Harriett BALLARD, deceased
Mrs. Eva SPENCE, removed
Mrs. Biddy WALLER, deceased

72

W. T. JOHNSTON, removed
Dr. & Mrs. Thomas STONE, removed
George B R. WALLER, deceased
Lazarus HALL, stricken off
Mrs. HALL, deceased
Willie WATERS, deceased
John H. KING, deceased
Robert DASHIELL, removed
Capt. BARCLAY, deceased
                              1852
William MURPHY, deceased
John JONES, deceased
William REDDISH, removed
Levy R. DRISKELL, removed
Mrs. Betsy DISHAROON, deceased
Bridget WALLER, deceased
Harriett BALLARD, deceased
Robert BAILY, deceased
George ATKINSON, deceased
                              1855
Levin WHITE of Monie, deceased
Mrs. Ann KING of Princess Anne removed to Baltimore
Mrs.Susan BOWLAND widow of Pr. Anne died
Mrs. Henry A. WHITE of Manokin,stricken off
William STEWART, died
Miss Juliania LONG d/o Littleton, removed.
Mrs. Henrietta ATKINSON of Almodington Manokin, dead.
Mrs. Matthias SPENCER of Old Academy removed to Easton Md.
Mrs. Julian CROSDALE removed to Washington City
Mrs. Eliza Anna MOORE, removed to Kentucky
Matthias ROBERTS, removed to Baltimore
Mrs. Cornelia ROBERTS, removed to Baltimore
James GIBSON, dead
Miss Ellen JOHNSTON, removed
Mrs. Aurelia DASHIELL, of Pr. Anne dead
Mrs. John COLLINS widow of Pr. Anne, removed
Mrs. Susan GILLIS, dead
Miss Ann Rebecca WHITE, removed
Miss Emily M. MOORE, removed
Charles S. SPENCER, removed
                              1856
Dr. Thomas JONES of Monie, removed
Miss Ellen WHITELOCK of Pr. Anne, removed
Charlotte E. ACWORTH w/o A. of Pr. Anne removed.
Robert Jenkins MARSHALL, removed
                              1857
Aurelia MILES w/o Alfred, dead
Dr. Littleton J. HANDY of "Waterloo" Monie, dead
Miss Amanda KENNERLY, removed
Adeline BYRD w/o W. J.BYRD, removed
                              1858
Dr. & Mrs. VALK of Westover, removed
Mrs. Margaret MOORE, dead
Sarah F. COVINGTON, dead
Isaac COVINGTON,stricken off

Leah Jane KING, removed
Annie KING w/o Henry, removed
Henrietta WARD w/o James, removed
Sarah JOHNSTON d/o W. W., dead
John P. MESSICK, removed
Lizzie WRIGHT removed to Memphis Tenn.
John HANDY, removed to Cambridge Md.
                                    1859
William Harrison DASHIELL, removed
Hugh R. E. MOORE, removed
Edward C. JONES, removed
                                    1860
Clara SPENCER, removed
Mary H. J. JENKINS, removed
Susan COURNAN, removed
Emma LUIDOW, removed
                                    1861
Amanda JONES, dead
Dr. Matthias SUDLER, dead
Francis DUNNAM, removed
                                    1862
Miss Ann B. R. WALLER d. 30 May 1876
Sallie E. M. WALLER now Mrs. Robert DASHIELL
Annie WALLER married lives in Baltimore
Mary Elin WALLER w/o Wm. T. died Jun 1883
George Arthur WOOLFORD, in Deleware
Miss Leah BEAUCHAMP d. 12 Aug 1865
Mr. Robert DASHIELL, suspended
Ellen DASHIELL died 14 Jul 1867
Rosina W. JOHNSTON died
John H. STEWART died 6 Nov 1855
Henrietta STEWART married Feb. 1874 lives in Baltimore
Mrs. SMITH, dead
Robert W. DOUGHERTY, removed Jan. 1865
Miss Amanda BOWLAND removed 1868
John MILLER removed to Baltimore 1872 returned Jul 1875
Mrs. Maria MILLER removed to Baltimore returned Jul 1875
John Samuel MILLER Sep 1864 ordained Deacon in Baltimore
Mrs. A. M. MILES removed Dec 1864
Mrs. Levin WHITE, married & removed
Mrs. Maria HOLBROOK, removed to Frederick Maryland
Miss Ellen HOLBROOK, removed to Frederick Md.
Edward H. HOLBROOK, removed to Frederick Md.
Thomas W. HOLBROOK removed Jan 1868 returned 1869
Mrs. Araminta HOLBROOK removed Jan 1868, returned 1869
J. Samuel HOLBROOK removed Jan 1868 died 25 Aug 1871
Mrs. Jennie W. DASHIELL removed to Baltimore 1865, returned
                    and died 14 April 1865
Miss Esther COTTMAN now Mrs. Dr. Henry BRISCOE removed to
                    Salisbury
Mrs. Elizabeth COTTMAN removed to Salisbury Md.
Littleton LONG Jr. removed to Baltimore
Henriett SUDLER removed to Louise Home Washington D.C. died
                                    1874
Joseph SUDLER removed to Baltimore died 25 Sep 1872

Mrs. Candace SUDLER removed to Baltimore
Mary A. WHITE removed to Washington
Miss Lizzie HYLAND married removed to Coventry Parish 1865
Miss Julie BAILY now Mrs. Berry T.J.B. JONES of Rock Creek
Mrs. A. H. JONES removed to Berlin Md.
Miss Julia JONES married removed to Kent Co. MD.
Mrs. Samuel B. D. JONES removed to Spring Hill Parish
Mrs. Julia KENNERLY removed to Spring Hill Parish
Mr. J. C. WANGEMAN, stricken off
Mrs. Virginia WANGEMAN, removed to Virginia
Miss Emily DASHIELL·removed to Virginia
Mrs. Thomas STONE removed to Missouri
Granville G. GARDNER, suspended
Miss Henrietta GARDNER, Mrs. Wm. J. BRITTINGHAM died 1866
Mrs. Lizzie WRIGHT, removed 1864
Miss Fannie ADAMS, removed to Alabama
Miss Eugenia ADAMS removed to Alabama
Rufus M. PARSONS removed to Baltimore
Miss Rozanna PARSONS removed to Baltimore
Mrs. Henrietta DENNIS, removed 1864
Miss Cerinda EVANS, removed
Mrs. Virginia DIXON now Mrs. Edward F. DUER
Mrs. Matilda DASHIELL removed to Annapolis Md.
Miss Esther Ann WILSON married J.F.A.TULL d.27 Aug 1866
Joseph H. SMITH removed to Atlanta Georgia
Sidney C. LONG, removed 1864
Mary HYLAND removed to Baltimore 1864
Miss Sarah H. WHITE, removed
Miss Louisa C. WHITE, removed
Mrs. Ann CHATTAM died Sep 1869
Ann PAGE, removed died February 1870
Arthur CRISFIELD removed to Portland Oregon
Mrs. Virginia E. NEWMAN removed to Baltimore and returned
Mrs. John R. STURGIS removed to New Town Md.
Miss Annie CROSDALE, married removed to Snow Hill Md
Miss Nannie Catherwood JONES, now Mrs. Samuel H. LANGFORD
Miss Virginia HYLAND, married removed to West Virginia
Winder H. HASTINGS, removed
Mrs. W. H. HASTINGS, removed
Mrs. Arthur CRISFIELD, removed to Chester town
Miss Sallie GILLIS, married Dr. James Stone & died
Mrs. Julia HEFFENSTEIN, removed 1864
John A. DASHIELL died 19 Nov 1865
Mrs. E. T. WAILES died 3 Sep 1866
Elizabeth ALice FOREMAN removed,returned & stricken off
Mrs. Anna Maria POTTER, removed, returned & stricken off
Miss Emily PRICE married George W. TYLER, removed
Samuel B. D. JONES removed to Spring Hill Parish
Miss Sarah W. DASHIELL now Mrs. G. G. GARDNER
Mrs. Elizabeth CAIN, removed
Miss Julia DASHIELL, removed to Baltimore
Ann Virginia MORRIS,removed,returned,married 17 June 1869
                    died 30 April 1873
Miss Sarah William BOUNDS removed March 1878 to Dorcester
                    County Maryland.

Miss Mary Ann COVINGTON,removed
Miss Georgianna WILLING, removed to Stepney Parish
Anna Irving HOLBROOK removed to Frederick Md. returned
Mary Anna COVINGTON, removed
Laura Virginia BRITTINGHAM married Thomas DIXON
Charlotte Emily BRITTINGHAM married George W. DIXON
Julia Constancia HERSEY removed to Spring Hill Parish
Sarah Hannah LANGFORD married William J. ANDERSON
Mrs. John A. BROWN, removed to Alabama
Miss METCALF, removed to Philadelphia
Miss H. M. LEIGH, removed
Joseph M. NEWMAN, removed to South Carolina
Miss Mary W. RIDER removed to Salisbury Md.
Jesse H. COVINGTON removed to Virginia
Mary E. MADDUX removed to Newtown Md.
Henry H. KENNERLY removed to Philadelphia
Samuel SUDLER removed to Kansas City Misouri
Samuel HUFTY and Mrs HUFTY removed to Philadelphia
Mrs. STAGG, removed to near NEWTOWN Md.
Mrs. James A. PEARCE, removed
Miss Minnie PEARCE, removed
                    1868
James Fairfax DASHIELL, removed to Baltimore
John Robert WILSON, removed to Texas
Miss Joseph RISLEY, removed
Ignatius W. PHOEBUS, died of yellow fever in Memphis 1875
Miss Fannie M. WHITE married Samuel S. SUDLER
Miss Mary Ann COVINGTON removed to Salisbury
Miss Eliza FREEMAN, removed
Mrs. John RIALL, removed
                    1870
George WILSON and wife, removed
Miss Irene DASHIELL, married Mr. CRAIG removed to Cambridge
                    1871
Rosalie DENNIS, married and removed
Clarence C. WALLER removed to Kirkwood Deleware
James ANDERSON, removed to Philadelphia died Dec 1875
Mrs. ANDERSON removed to Philadelphia
Mirs HICKMAN removed to Philadelphia
Miss Jennie THOMAS married Joseph M. NEWMAN removed to S.
                    Carolina
Dr. Henry BRISCOE died 2 April 1878
Mrs. Margaret Ann BROOKS, removed to Pennsylvania
Harry Thomas HARDING removed to Philadelphia
Miss Ellen WILSON,married Clarence C. WALLER removed to Del.
James t. HEARN, removed to Newtown Md.
Mrs. Leah A. HEARN removed to Newtown Md.
Emeline E. MUIR removed to Baltimore
Miss Mary Anne E. HEATH married Sydney Revell
Sarah Martha YOUNG, removed
Annie CHATTAM married Richard J. SMITH
                    1874
Thomas T. BOULDIN died 31 Jul 1875
Mrs. Clara H. BOULDIN, removed
J. Lewis LOGAN, removed

1876
Mrs. Virginia Catherine MUIR, died
1880
Eleanor Elizabeth Ann DASHIELL married Archie M. WALLER
1885
James F. BRITTINGHAM, removed to Pocomoke City
Miss Virginia BROWN, removed
Mrs. Ada DASHIELL, removed
Miss Esther DASHIELL, removed
Mrs. Sallie Brown DASHIELL, died 1886
Mrs. Emma E. DOUGHERTY, removed
Sallie Elzey DENNIS, removed
Nannie DENNIS, insane
Joseph Emory NEWMAN, removed
Miss Nellie Eva FURNISS transfered to Trinity Church Tiffin
     Ohio
Mrs. Sallie W. GARDNER, removed
Granville Graham GARDNER, removed
Miss Nellie GILLIS HOLBROOK d. 30 Aug 1887
Ida HUGHES, removed
William Edgar JONES transferred to Grace Church
Mrs. Maria M. JONES transferred to Grace Church
Mrs. Julia Ann JONES, now Mrs. D. DAVIS, to Grace Church
Mrs. Martha Ann LEWIS died December 1886
Miss Mary Edith MILBOURN, removed
Miss Adeline MILES, dead
Mrs. Alice Florence NOBLE died July 1887
Mrs. Marguerite OATES, removed
Miss Annie Elzey OATES, removed.
Mrs. Mary Ann WALLER removed to Grace Church
Clarence C. WALLER, removed
Miss Ellen WALLER, removed
James STEVENS, dead
Elizabeth UPSHUR died August 1887

< continue from prev page >

81

< continue from prev page >

< continue from prev column >

www.ingramcontent.com/pod-product-compliance
Lightning Source LLC
LaVergne TN
LVHW051704080426
835511LV00017B/2727